Mantras and Musical Solutions

Mantras and Musical Solutions

Imaginative Chemistry and Transformative Intent

ANDREW FRANCK

iUniverse, Inc.
Bloomington

Mantras and Musical Solutions
Imaginative Chemistry and Transformative Intent

iUniverse books may be ordered through booksellers or by contacting:

iUniverse
1663 Liberty Drive
Bloomington, IN 47403
www.iuniverse.com
1-800-Authors (1-800-288-4677)

ISBN: 978-1-4620-3934-0 (sc)
ISBN: 978-1-4620-3937-1 (ebk)

Printed in the United States of America

iUniverse rev. date: 09/13/2011

TABLE OF CONTENTS

Remembering the Present Tense

Projections and Nuptial Chamber

Assembling the Artifactual Spirit 163

The Atmosphere of Chemical Intent

As the precursor of modern day science and psychology, alchemy labored since ancient times by means of fathoming *gesture* throughout the whole of the natural world. Gesture in this context refers to the inner causes and essential characteristics substance expresses through its multiform states of solid, liquid, gas, mineral, vegetable, animal, including the human being. Alchemy's aim evolved from the premise that the physical world, the psyche and spirit are inextricably connected. The practitioner of the Royal Art, as alchemy was often referred to, was on a path of conscientious awareness regarding the meaning of phenomena and the soul-spirit forces animating the world. If it could survey present-day science, alchemical sensibility would contend that the elements and compounds presently discerned by sense-bound thinking are basically corpses, in effect, waste products of living or once-living organisms of mother earth; chemistry's one-sided approach to matter abstracts, shapes and routinely forces the dross of substance to behave solely through physical reactions. While this kind of efficiency has its certain practical value, alchemical practice on the other hand, whether it involved transmuting one substance into another or one imagination into another, strove to comprehend and direct nature and psyche through sublime creative purpose. Intending to reveal spirit in matter, the Art would gradually bestow upon the practitioner insight into the workings of creation. Significantly, on this road of higher purpose alchemy would make many new discoveries regarding the physical world. The Art would shed light on the overall context in which knowledge can reveal the workings of the universe. Its achievements wouldn't impede the intellectual fruits won by careful observation and experiment; rather, history has shown just the opposite.

Materially and psychologically, alchemy recognized the idea of transmutation as a working fact intent upon producing a universal transmuting agent identified as the philosophic stone, the *lapis philosophorum*. The stone was envisioned as a catalytic vehicle

1

enabling the formless void of the *prima materia*, the potential within matter, to evolve substance into its exalted essence. While the *prima materia* was postulated as base matter, the void was considered the *will* within creation itself. The philosophic stone represented an oscillating current enabling the soul of the searcher to illuminate into the void while enabling matter to transmute into a noble, even moral, state. Alchemy's inspirational effort to create the *lapis* invited basic forces and materials into a distillation, uplifting their terrestrial condition through cosmological principles of higher organization while elevating a substance's individualized *meaning*. In so doing, alchemy sought to touch the veils of matter and uncover the significance of phenomena beyond the ordinarily perceived. Those veils are in fact conditioned by the senses, which necessarily structure and weave surface upon meaning in order to enable *physical* perception. Physical perception is the condition for material experience as well as the latent condition for "freeing" creation from terrestrial determination. This physical-sensible circumstance requires a context for maintaining sight of the spirit else it corrodes, densifying experience into misshapen soul forces and superficial imagery. By transmutation, purification and intent, through uncovering meaning inherent in creation, the Ardent, the practitioner of the Art, dissolves those materially bound impediments that darken sensibility, consciousness and understanding while uncovering the depths of cosmic creativity. The Ardent enables this uncovering through the stages of his own enlightenment, marrying each new *solution* in his quest toward ever-clearer intentions. The path was known as the Great Work. Given proper direction, the practitioner's effort yielded the transparent underpinnings of nature, eliciting meaning within manifestation. In all its mystery and worth, the realization of the philosophic stone was a demonstration of creative effort displaying enlightened intent.

• • • •

The alchemical researcher, who preceded both chemist and psychologist, projected into matter's dark mystery the search for the Self, the archetypal center and organizing principle of personality. The essence of fluid individuality was symbolized by the spirit of Mercury-Hermes-Thoth. The *lapis philosophorum,* the agent that could outwardly transform base metals into gold as well as heal sickness, became essential to this quest; the lapis became a transformational tool for evolving the soul and matter towards a fructification that frees both into the Atmosphere of earned creative capacity and wisdom.

By investigating matter and how it behaves, clues from the outer world—phenomena—revealed insights into the microcosm, the inner world of the body-soul-self resplendently structured out of the cosmos. The Ardent engaged chemical transformations in order to reveal metabolic, unconscious motives housed within the crucible of the work, as well as the vessel of his own being. The *lapis* requires preparation, distillation, purification by the *nigredo* (blackening), the *albedo* (whitening), the *citrinitas* (yellowing), and the *rubedo* (reddening). Each stage begins with a decay process and ends with rebirth. A chemical wedding, a transformational synthesis, would display the evolving inner *and* outer worlds at each stage.

To begin, the mood of the Ardent required devotion: the practitioner knows that he yearns, yet cannot clearly envision the fruit of this longing. Nevertheless, his will for a truer vision of himself and the world are paramount. Here, within his body-soul is a "facsimile" of the *prima materia*, the "first matter," the "orphan," the "chaos found in filth." From this is glimpsed what devotion can be devoted to: *that* out of which all creation begins, forms, sustains, and sacrifices in order to become fully realized.

Matter in its states of earth, air, fire, and water conducts the *prima materia* within substance. Purifying matter amounted to reorganizing the proportion of formative forces—ethers—of those elements, fructifying them until they matched those of the most noble, royal and light-filled substance, gold. Purifying the soul amounted to destroying the baser nature of sense-bound perception and material-bound thinking by visiting the interior, the inner Arcanum, the inner *mysterium*. The Arcanum is the mystery of generative force. To behold the Arcanum the truth of creation as *given within* the body requires apprehending the will awakening her more spiritualized condition. Here, whitening is symbolized by the phoenix hatching from the once unconscious lunar egg into an evolved personality capable of cosmically heightened Imagination.

The Work pauses after the Ardent completes these primary stages of the *prima materia*'s transformation. At this stage in the *citrinitas*, the Ardent soul readies to sacrifice the structure of his being to the true opus, spirit-gold-enlightenment. The Ardent suspends into the work, palpably receiving Mercury descending from the heavens, the god's wings of ether bringing him through the spheres of the planets, through the conditions of Old Saturn's warmth, Old Sun's air and Old Moon's waters. Here, the Ardent's transformative capacity incarnates purified motives into substance through his developed will. Mercury appears through the spherical nature of fluids, the mutable metal quicksilver, the rejuvenating will and the self-fertilizing cosmic serpent, *ouroboros*. Mercury is the messenger of light, the carrier of the Christ impulse, the archetypal Self combining opposites; he is a transformer as well as heaven's reflection in nature. By carrying the wave of chemical-ether, through cosmic music Mercury animates the bodily condition of soul. Purified, this enlivening quickens outside consciousness first in the world of the senses. Substance begins to transform, being no longer "stuff." Matter is spirit-gesture made available to sensation in a wholly new way.

Further distilled, the purified self no longer looks back at the enchanting womb of the unconscious, no longer identifies with the old knowledge of the senses. There is no returning. On the way toward the third *coniunctio*, the soul again visits the interior, now going backwards in time to meet itself in the condition of its functional life-body, the metabolism of its youth. Here the soul must grasp that the living force of renewal must marry the moral consciousness of spirit. Past and future are re-membered in the present tense; the body serves its spirit and soul through its existence in the material world. Within the potential for self-renewal and resurrection, *manas*, *buddhi* and *atman* (Vedic terms for the elevated bodies of consciousness) ready to actualize as higher aspects of the human being as sense process evolves perception in cosmic light.

The multicolored iridescence of the *cauda pavonis*, the peacock's tail, signals the transition into a fourth stage, the dawn-like reddening or *rubedo* of love. Spring arrives and with it consciousness participates in the stirring of the world-unconscious. Nature's life forces are no longer strange to the Ardent. The seeds within earth stir, dreaming the blossom and fruit. The green lion, the sulfuric aspect of Mercury, devours what's left of the confused soul, again dividing sun and moon, but now within his digestive tract as he dies into a new life. This heralds the ultimate test and final loss for the Ardent: Can the conscious self, having met the forces of nature and spirit, having come so far and sacrificed so much, now give the fruits of the Work up to the collective light of humanity? Can the self serve as the true vessel for world transformation? Can this knowledge be offered without self-appointed ambitions?

If through this trial the Ardent breaks through his egotism, the unwavering fire of the fourth degree hatches the divine child, the *filius philosophorum*: reconciling self-will with the cosmos. The *prima materia*'s four elements evolve though the soul into Mercury's manifestations throughout the organic, inorganic, and spiritual worlds. Into *Sol* and *Luna* then into the unified *lapis*, the goal of active creation reaches its embryonic completion. The Ardent now assists the cosmos in two final operations: the *multiplicatio* and the *projectio*, in which the Self, the genuine *lapis*, projects and multiplies by changing inner experiences into gold, supra-consciousness. Illumined by the self that once projected only the partly conscious personality, the Ardent attains inward stillness in order to *deliver* the music of the cosmos into the radiance of the *Potent Body*, the dynamic higher self. Specified within conscious endeavor but beyond consciousness is the divinely manifest *coniunctio*—the Self transfiguring into a clear, incorruptible, eternally living form emanating a peach-blossom hue: the *quintessentia*, the fifth element. Derived from the four elements in the vessel of substance and personality, consciousness marries its cosmological legacy, birthing the planetary motives that can only arise from the toil of Creation's own created. This is the vehicle the cosmos has awaited—the Unknown—from where creation's source will be directed by the love required to continue the cosmos. From here flows the tincture unto eternity, the creative essence providing the solvent, fire, and passion for evolving the cosmos. This *lapis* in the body of the Ardent is truth and wisdom, knowledge and spirit extracted from matter now activated as spirit-substance. The Ardent understands that each element, every species, all motives exist within him. *As outside, so within*: a reformulation from Hermes' *Emerald Tablet* is the key to conceiving the new world-becoming, the New Arcanum.

Out of the listening capacity for the music of the spheres, the Ardent with his living stone shines. He is the higher work, the higher Self sculpted into matter speaking the melody of how creation *will be*. Distilled out of unconscious instinct, the work was first begun from a context of inherent soul immaturity. Gradually, the demonstration of Self entered the realm of the divine by a crystalline image of wholeness. Embodied as moral consciousness itself, the Ardent transforms into a new kind of human being, the fruit of Creation, ready to sacrifice for the whole to gain illumination.

• • • •

Mantras As Alchemical Solutions

Soul displays insides, *content*, wherever its manifestation, whatever its endeavor. The work of alchemy supports the display of the soul where fixed or stagnated sensibility no longer serves the higher self, where perception must rise to the supersensible, where light touches substance becoming the fabric of Imagination. For alchemical sensibility, *form* is the vehicle appearing out of what appearance means, while transparent to what essence means to say. In other words, *how* the spiritual is revealed is by way of addressing the meaning through intentional work, whether it is scientific, technical, artistic or psychological. Alchemy's elusiveness, obscurity and cryptic sensibility belie the nature of an experience that cannot simply be translated through the patterns of the ordinarily known. Symbol and allegory pull the nature of communication much closer to the world of Imagination by asking the senses and cognitive faculties to perceive, respond and behave differently.

For alchemical sensibility, the *lapis* projects elevated purpose into the material of ordinary metals with its capacity to metamorphose them into gold. How should we interpret this faculty of the Stone? When darkness is illumined by awareness, its savagery evolves into enthusiasm, warm intention from flesh. The striving self changes the products of the unconscious and is in turn changed by the effort. Gold not only symbolizes but is of the nature of illumined soul forces and exalted substances. The alchemical idea of the *proiectio* points to the Stone's power to convert base metals and unconscious content into gold, higher consciousness. The collective unconscious has within it the capacity to transform into the collective beauty of body-soul-spirit, humankind made concretely divine, sacred. Alchemical completion is prefigured historically and psychologically in Hermes Trismegistus' *Emerald Tablet*, the Chinese *Diamond Body* and the Buddhist *Dharmakaya*. Implicit in these ancient texts is the presentation of the enlightened self promoted to the realm of creative spirit. Together with these cosmic Principalities, the practitioner's higher self activates the capacity for evolving the universe into a New Atmosphere vivified from the depths of loving intent.

As the realm of perception is anchored within the soul's abilities to *experience*, alchemy involves a heightened functioning of psyche, how the soul takes up spiritual causation, transforming itself and matter within the context of the physical world. While the soul is the active agent for transformative work, it is functionally anchored within the body and the senses, endeavoring to make sense of the outer environment as well as the inner realms of sensation, emotion and thought. In alchemical terminology, the psyche may be rarified or distilled by certain motives that make sublime the coarser aspects of consciousness and matter. By elevating the sense for cosmic purpose and *artifactual* vision, the psyche by way of the *consciousness soul* educates the inner conduct necessary for realizing these intentions. The transformative agency of the soul sheds light on the unconscious through its portal from the supra-conscious, the spiritual. The soul as well congeals scattered attention through coagulating the fragments of the chaotic mind bringing clearer intent to vague, distorted desires. Through the contours of purposive imagery, the soul's own sensual "tissue" animates and educates sensibility. Through the capacity of individualized imagination, soul progressively reveals more and more of itself and its activity. Within its own vessel, its alembic, the soul as matrix of "inner" and "outer" Imagination works to marry chthonic with celestial motives, bringing together imagery and significance. Alchemical imagination develops this capacity of soul, giving imagination the direction required for meeting the divine. As well, alchemical sensibility addresses the fundamental nature of sense and substance through the archetypal polarities of light and dark, heaviness and imponderability, sulfur and salt. Nature's workings can be addressed and redressed to enable the practitioner to elevate and fructify consciousness as well as the natural world. Through hermetic intentionality, transformative aptitude increases through the facilities of rhythm and relationship, perception (the sense bath) and cognition (the distillate). Alchemy engages within the polarity of the amorphous (sulfur) and the crystallizing (salt); its practice invokes the transformative power of the metamorphic drop-forming agency of Hermes-Mercury-Thoth, the god-messenger. With will force and pictorial representation, Mercury mediates the physical and ethereal by functionally applying and integrating the principles of heaven and earth.

Through the alchemical art, the practitioner's character developed through working with processes that require taking up and re-visioning cosmic and terrestrial intent. A mythic theme—a projective *mysterium*—could be generated through specifying the participant's own development; the practicing of one's character generated the path for developing soul content as well as the ability to engage substance in ways required for understanding and conceivably healing the cosmos. Alchemy's adepts felt that if the structure of imagination were spiritually and physically aligned to the cosmos' higher intent and motivated by clarity of meaning, the soul's higher purposes could fructify certain "arrested" worldly elements. How will forces could gain embodiment, how substances could transmute with intentional processes, how the soul might develop consciously were tangible issues enabling the spiritual display of meaning in the physical realm. Accordingly, the art of alchemy became a higher level of soul-making, ardently realigning the material of nature by using the *self* as the primary artifact. This self-artifact lives as a time-marriage freely manifested through one's individuality guided by the book of nature and the sense for the divine. The essence of alchemy reveals the true reality and true nature of the Ardent as one who practices purified intent, reaching for the heightened consciousness of Imagination, Inspiration and Intuition.

••••

Numerous ideas in *Mantras and Musical Solutions* take their inspiration from those earlier psycho-metallurgists' endeavors. Herein is a panoramic approach to the royal marriage, the *Coniunctio*, embracing alchemical effort to sift and shape soul and substance, embracing the creative principle within the Art while peeling away veils of fixated imagery regarding substance, force, cause, effect. Morphologically (and anamorphically) these mantric pictures cultivate and add to both the "sense bath" and "distillate" of the alchemical art. Each mantra has been fermented out of hermetic history, distilling a new context for psychic extraction, seeking to amplify and project the soul's capacity for Imagination. By dissolving and congealing imagery, projecting mythos, memory and motive, the mantric phrase takes on the function of a sense-distillate meant to dissolve abstractions and habits within the ordinary bandwidth of impressions; to porously open experience to meaning, to saturate and deepen comprehension. Through this imaginal gesturing of essence within substance, the materially bound image-concept is suspended, and here, through the span of seven elocutionary movements, to be envisioned as the spiritually concretized, the flesh made heavenly as the heavenly is made flesh. Imagining soulfulness is thus a *meta*-observation, an inner-sight, made available through the activity of transformative work. Through *psychoemblematic* imagery the practitioner steps into and appreciates the sensibilities of those early adventurers of the Art as well as directly experiencing substance and gesture unveiling their meaning.

The Sanskrit word *mantra* consists of the root *man*—"to think" (as in *manas*, mind) and the suffix—*tra*, designating tools or instruments; thus, a literal translation would be "instrument of thought." Mantras are phrases that, since Vedic times, are considered capable of creating transformation, healing, peace, illumination and good will. Many spiritual traditions have long since used prayers and repetitive phrases as a way of connecting to the divine; their recitation is often believed to be crucial to the maintenance and existence of the cosmos. Conscientiously and actively joined to divine motives, these sound emanations express their intent through a distilled mode of speaking. They articulate the potency of word-substance, motivating a subtle field whose effects may gradually be assimilated into the depths of the individual's soul organization. As such, mantras (and inspired prayers) are rays of intent affirming significant connections to and from the spiritual world while engendering new capacities within the soul. This kind of "wording" is akin to a distillate, a solution of purified intent. The devotional breath of the mantra dances between heaven and earth, sound and silence.

An even deeper sense of mantras reveals their function as word-bodies, living aural gestures of spiritual form. Permeated with right effort and good will, these word-bodies influence the interpenetrative process in the circuit between human intent and divine will. Through the *etheric* power of the mantra, human and divine motives meet in a context of higher purpose, right thinking, feeling and right action. In the East, mantras are typified by the sacred *AUM*, the intoned font of all mantras. *AUM* is the primordial vibration and manifestation of Brahman, the creative source before and beyond all existence. In the West, with its own characteristic relationship to the sense world, mantras at times have taken on the form of aphorisms, having their own special word-nature. The thinking within aphorism undergoes a particular kind of filtering process. In aphorism there is a distillation of a thought into the concentrated statement. This concentrated statement functions then as the *activity* revealing the thought's vital meaning and force. From the mind's noumenal distillate a *coagulation* occurs from within the psyche, yielding an essential phrase of soul. Wonderful examples of this are found in the words of Heraclitus, Novalis, Goethe, de Chazal and Nietzsche.

On the level of the discursive intellect, aphorism may present certain difficulties since "conclusions" are arrived at without apparently illustrating the process for reaching them. Though aphorisms appear as conclusive statements, they live as "solutions" meant to activate and enliven character and resolve. In aphorism, the revelation of a general truth or insight contains the challenge of a contextual atmosphere; the phrase's intent determines the self-evidence and pertinence regarding *what* is revealed, to whom it is directed and for what purpose. For the author, the words themselves have been *solved* through cognitive *fermentation*, through his own sifting of the essentials while expelling the dross. For the prepared or disposed reader, the aphorism lives as something immediate, intensifying contemplation and savoring the theme's scope, worth and application.

As living word-bodies, mantras display a current of effects from the field of meaning through the factual organs of larynx, ear, skeleton *and* soul; these evoke a raying forth from the depths of the human to the divine. Mantras dynamically enable inner articulation of feeling to sound into the outer exigencies of form. Though traditionally repetitive, mantras may also conduct their wisdom *in the moment*, whereby their sounding amplifies the Imagination, the soul faculty of spiritual endeavor. As essentially distilled statements, the aphorisms in *Mantras and Musical Solutions* intend to carry a *cosmologic* cell, a vital imprint of the Bride, the Alchemical Muse. As articulated in my earlier book, *The Transparent Bride*, the devoted seeker of the spirit, the Ardent, pursues wisdom herself, the Bride, who lives throughout the manifestations of creation, rarified yet in fact wholly evident. The aim of the Ardent is to "see" the *gestural* world's transparent causes, to re-imagine and guide world evolution through the wisdom-filled endeavor of the Bride within the World-Soul. He devotes himself to making the "atmosphere" anew by enabling its *re-limbing* through love and right intent. The Ardent risks enigma and riddle in order to access the motives of substance, psyche and spirit. By separating, fermenting, coagulating and extracting matters of soul, nature, even the social fabric, the Ardent "works" the Bride's intent, cooks the Imagination's vapors which can then be freely uttered through aphorism and mantra. By this effort, the Ardent invites higher purpose into the imagination and transformation of matter, distilling the sensual cause of body into a spiritually evolved *mysterium* of the new Atmosphere, the *Potent Body*.

The aphorisms and mantras in *Mantras and Musical Solutions* mean to stretch the membrane of their own aspiration, overtly bringing to light features and qualities of the Unseen, of substance, sensing, willing, cognition, feeling, spirit. For some ears these *mantric* "solutions" will resound with wit and probity, even insight into cosmological process. For others, they'll wax occult with their hermetic underpinnings regarding the world of elements, or inferences regarding preternatural force within substance. Nonetheless, though filled with resolve, they never mean to be imperious. They invite whoever warmly pursues the mysterious relationship between wisdom and substance; they engage whoever is a genuine cosmopolite devoted to the visible manifestations of the divine, the *theophanics* of soul. For this kind of devotion, one must have a profound faith in the causal *Bodies* of nature, those beings heavenly transparent and factual. Whoever is dedicated to this endeavor becomes more enthused within this circuit of engagement, and through this their wonder lives ignited by luminous Imagination, charged with what life and the cosmos mean to reveal through purified motives. In the vapors of authentic and distilled speech, the ardent reader may imagine himself on a transformative journey into a transparent condition, an *Atmosphere* meant to attract and be moved by the causal beauty of conscientious human creation. As the ardent self apprehends the possibility of this atmosphere, the soul embraces the Bride, Sophia-Wisdom herself, enthused through vital contact within the mysteries of matter and spirit. Within mantra, conducting evolution through active wisdom, the Ardent stands nakedly factual as a celebrant announcing his wedding to a sacred and *refreshable* world.

A Chemical Song

The nature of infinity is this: That everything has its Own Vortex, and when once a traveler thro' Eternity has pass'd that Vortex, he perceives it roll backwards behind his path into a globe itself infolding like a sun.

—William Blake

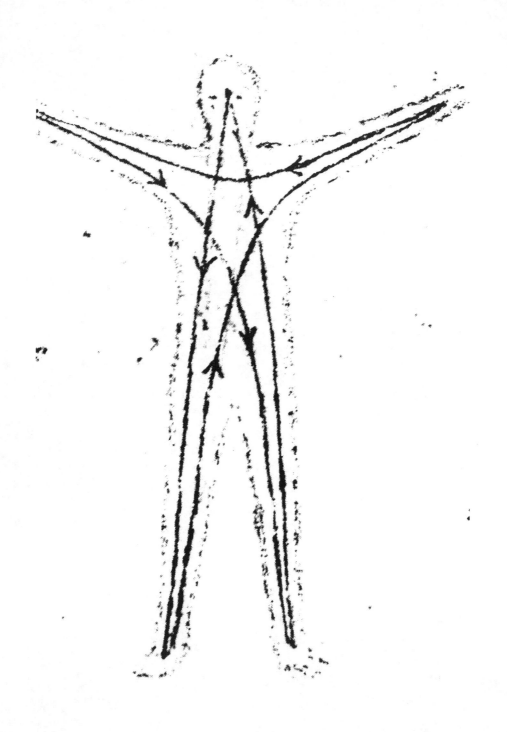

The Architecture of Devotion

Before the conditions for substance, intention emanates chemical wisdom. Chemistry streams the world periphery gathering life into material condensation. As life ignites from synapses of wisdom, the chemical gifts display the body as the architecture of devotion.

•

The Divine Embrace Pulls By Fire

As original vitality, fire eagerly sends its substance outward, point pulled toward periphery, a center inverting, spreading into space. Space secretes through the body of warmth; circulation escapes the dimensional tether.

•

Physical Universe

By the agency of time, a ripening of formative force elicits the world of substance. As substance, the physical universe is the imagination of primal heat spatially extended.

•

Not Unlike a Skull of Unlimited Size

Pulled from the oscillating currents of intent, clothed in obscurity, moving the drive within life, the metabolism houses the primary Ignition—its *body* of warmth metamorphosing into forces from cosmos inward. Formed in order to be spent, the cosmos evaporates into its secondary display, *blue* into blue, its image becoming not unlike a skull of unlimited size.

•

On Heat

Reflecting force while organizing negative pressure, warmth interpenetrates from the far reaches of universal space into telluric dispersal. As the earth condenses structure from form, individualized substance exhibits the differing states of heat. Cooling into substance elicits sub-planetary gesturing tracing cosmic cause.

•

The Skin of Transparence

Before creation, the *not-yet* emanated warmth. How warmth would express could only be revealed through the metamorphosis of time venturing into air process. This *would-be* excites time as creation itself pours through the skin of transparence.

•

Warmth Production

Reflection generates attraction, attraction projects *active* heat. Throughout time, matter houses the origin of divided warmth . . . and the effects of warmth suppression.

•

Who Can Afford To Sacrifice?

What is breath if not a lung to become? What is sound if not the *heard* by the pre-attentive ear? *Who, what* is capable of sacrifice?

•

Identity, the Organ of Substance

The self was destined to be the organ of perception. Toward the organ of selfhood, the Arcana extracts the force of Saturn, projecting light from the sphere of emptiness. This orients the origin of origins while anticipating the elixir of freely decayed autonomy begun prior to time.

·

A Warp Was Laid

A warp was laid into which the time slough was braided. Accordingly, conflating will with wisdom, duration became a necessity for cosmological unfolding, principally *all* unfolding.

·

Key to Heaven

As the cosmos opens towards the creation of heart, heavenly warmth forms a bud within the center of that which will become the blood's circulation.

·

First Emanation

When the poise within existence constructed the tonus for life, there, from the elocutionary force of the first *matter*, the word emanated the dream of the human being.

•

Time

Imaginative *shape* modulates the life of motives as the chemical condition individuates, extended by the ethers separating. As vacuum relates to mass, *form* relates to chemical suspension. Motives are loosed while the inconceivable waits.

•

Capillary Motion

By multiplying warmth the chemical-charge ignites, increasing new capillaries for the potential of body. From Purusha, from Adam Caedman, the cosmic spaces seek earthly momentum *for* human being.

•

The Projective Cross

The purpose and aim of evolution is the human being. Substances however are needed for this being to materialize. The cosmic activity necessary for achieving human being is substantively demonstrated by an axis illustrating four polarities divisible by three. Herein the body, the senses and the world find their basis.

•

Pneumatic Circuit

As light condenses from tone, so tone from life. The ethers evolve from the *unheard-of,* pausing within the atmosphere. Readdressing the cosmic dream within breathing, tone into life suffers by suspension into sensation; life from tone endures intent within solution.

•

Atma

Throughout the conditions of warmth, reflected heat draws form. Form draws air. From the warmth-atmosphere the ether issues the rhythm of primary breath. *Pneuma* expressing Osiris whole, Isis copulating.

•

Magnification Steps Into Vacuum

The duality within Wisdom's egg allows for introducing movement into silence. When inversion takes place in the ether, *magnification* steps into vacuum. With the ensuing vacancy, a secondary, inconceivable womb awaits.

•

Magnifying the Primary Display

Quantity and integer are constituted by a derivative warmth contracting the *formal bodies* while magnifying the primary display. Here, "the inner proportions of the *I* are exactly mirrored as unconscious proportions in the astral sphere."

Multiplication and Ignition

As the expeller rays of decayed warmth grew mindful, the universal solvent became the potential for dissolution through creation. As the force of emanation contributes to the conditions of condensation, whatever spent grew flushed, ready, dreamful, ardent.

•

Emanation

What else but the enthusiasm can ignite? What else but the circulation can multiply? By creating space geometric form unfolds grace, pouring out substance. In this unheard stillness opens the egg of sung albumin, with a vacuum for its yolk.

•

From Sphere to Infinity

By the origins of warmth, the embryonic Adam Caedmon extends light into viscera. Elongating the skull, he reaches infinity through the force of his limbs.

•

Chronicling the Body

All body arises from a spherical source whose measure is a globe lengthened. The body is the deepest imagination, a drawn-out expression enduring the structure of the entire cosmos.

•

Sense and Reflex

For soul to experience the world, percepts require condensation, perceptions necessitate refraction. As sentient reflex, the *astrum* is born.

•

Cosmic Nerve

As the sum of Saturn traces its urge, the cosmic substance of nerve dies into body. To die into matter was the magnificent exhaustion initiated by nerve.

•

What is the Eye Worth?

Archetypal aim authorizes logic. Intention surrenders to causal vision, its projection follows the structure of purposive course. Throughout surface, primal aim turns toward sense, sense into the primacy of "other." What is the cosmos worth? What is the eye worth? These are questions of surface and sacrifice.

•

A Fulcrum for Oxidation

When air married the expeller rays of carbon it positioned itself a fulcrum from which the world oxidized its sounds.

•

Ethers, Elements, Spirit Marrow

Born from spirit, dying into form, elemental substance emanates perceptivity, doing so while pneumatically the *physiology* of the elements surfaces below the horizon of experience. The ethers intone and articulate through primordial silence. As the ethers emanate substance, substance emerges, triumphal, needy, filled with urge and relation.

•

Silence Is A Metaphor for Substance

In the seeming of silence there is nevertheless two sounds. Careful listening first reveals a high frequency which is the nervous system emitting its neurological drone. The second is a low rumble, the blood circulating. In actuality there is no silence. Silence exists as repose intended by the soul. As intention converging, silence is a metaphor for the condition of substance available through the transit of soul.

•

Tone and Perspective

Through archetypal yearning pneumatic rhythm is born between meaning and projection. By examining intent growing porous, the potent noise of touching the periphery with infinite limbs resounds.

The music of the *astrum* erases sound to access the unheard.
As melody into matter, the breath itself wanders, wafting in the rhythm between feeling and wonder. The breath overrides the opacity of petrified sensing. By freeing breathing, what does the freed air create?

When body is joined to tone, yearning has come to rest. The invisible tongue tastes the music of the *not-yet*. Before all bodies, the tongue reaches for the life of things.

Within the physiology of hearing lies the assimilation of timbre, the accumulation of suggestion, the projection of rareness and design—the daimon realm.

By the cadence of metamorphosis, through hearing comes *interest*. In obtaining the gifts of the ear the will moves toward comprehension.

The relation of concentration to hearing comes about through bone conduction, through the iron force within conduction. The skeleton displays the concentrate of heavenly form. Concentration mirrors primary matter.

Restlessness is made known through tone *inside* the bones.

The fall into tone is a falling out of metabolism. Tones hold jurisdiction over nature and over those who are who are themselves subjects of nature. But not over those no longer subject to Nature.

Together, invention and stillness coalesce in the sensitivity for tone.

Succinctly, what can the *listened to* afford to sacrifice? Post-eidetic coagulation?

Coaxing rhythms into resolution, binding elegantly all cadences, in its present condition, the body prepares for the experimental music.

Inflammations from the future offer the perspective of archetypal hysteria.

Music is an inflammation from the future longing for the cosmos' true ears, its true speech. Music is the principle by which solutions gain rationale and make sense, the mutable string on which tone glides is the character of the cosmos. Music enjoins the dead to approach the living.

As music demonstrates accumulated memory, melody articulates through remembering the future.

Remembering the future, time involutes into sense.

Whispering with archetypal sensitivity, the body refines the corpse.

Spirit is the threshold hovering, watching—reverberating into center from periphery. Density inheres as the microcosm's tone inflects all about. As the sound wells into phantom bellies, the presence releases into exuberance.

•

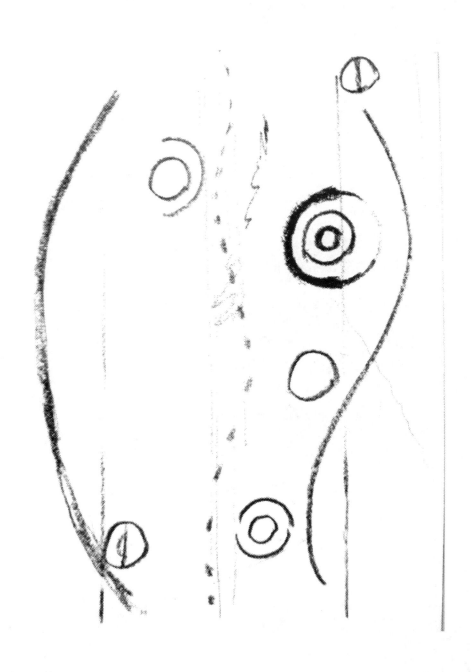

The Atmosphere

There is nothing in creation created or born that does not reveal its inner form outwardly as well, for the internal always works toward revelation.

—Jacob Boehme

In the Beginning

The concept of *beginning* must itself be open to causation through the aptitude *from* and *for* nothingness. If in the beginning life and death were not yet separate, how then would there be a beginning?

•

Saturn Effect

All heads complete their formation through an extended feat of Saturn. The head then represses Saturn forces, fashioning the transparent into circumstance, impression and fact.

•

The Skull Within the Head

The orb having the power from which is conceived *relation* is a very secret fixative.

•

Tonality In the Unheard

As the cosmic thirst for factual tongue and ears, musical impulse erases the unheard-sound, enervating into speech, tone, substance. By the powers of Will, the cosmos dreams that which cannot be wholly predicted yet must be projected. Through *characterization*, heaven seeks intimacy in projection, seeks the unheard tonality of the unimaginable. Projectively, life inheres in the matrix of sound, as wisdom coagulates the destiny of affection.

•

Assembling Aspiration

Through a solution of silica, light informs physical necessity, forming the pre-perceptible vision. In crystallization the emanating eye meets the horizon of the *unseen*.

•

Magnum Mysterium

Describing the condition of the cosmos before manifestation, *iliaster* is the term Paracelsus uses when referring to the great universal matrix, the condition of pure potentiality. This potentiality is to be imagined as a seed from which the universe was germinated. In order to initiate manifestation, *iliaster* divides, developing the *mysterium magnum,* an invisible spiritual force projecting primordial matter as the basis of all that is begotten. Further dissolving itself, the sacrifice of *iliaster* projects the opposition of One and the Other. Paracelsus specifies the One as strictly *iliaster* and the Other *aquaster.* The *ilaster* is a fiery, active principle; the *aquaster* a watery, passive principle. In each human being both are simultaneously at work. The *magnum mysterium* links spirit and matter into an indissoluble whole, yet the *prima materia* within it seeks "redemption," the wish of the spirit to become visible in the sacred eye of the chemical marriage.

•

Primacy of Spirit

Craving begins paradoxically from the primacy of pure somatic devotion, the cosmic discharging out of itself. Through porous intent, the endeavor of spirit projects motion throughout stillness, stillness in motion.

•

Releasement

Sense-residue inheres by the skin of appearance. By way of sensing Spirit, surface ignition *increases* reflexively, rhythmically increasing inner tension in the quest for comprehending the aeriform. By the force of the Sun, as air contracts, its intervals claim tone. As the life-ether inducts the chemical, the physiology releases its transparence.

•

Prima Materia

As the *ouroboros* encircling world periphery, blood motions the afterimage of spirit. In this light, blood is to be understood as the tangible origin of substances.

•

Carbon Path

Life evaporates into water and condenses into carbon. With evaporation life disappears in appearance, with condensation appearance draws out the end point of life. To elaborate, the quantity of carbonic acid breathed out in a single day is considerable; a human being exhales over two pounds of carbonic acid daily, half a pound of this is solid carbon, charcoal. In the course of a year, the average person breathes out approximately two hundred pounds of charcoal, considerably more than his or her weight. Whether an elephant or a gnat, a butterfly or a bird, all breathe into the world carbonic acid gas.

·

First Space Process

The cranium is wisdom salted; the organs, planetary motives adjusted; the limbs, love magnified. Extended from its primordial source, the body is the original space process.

·

Second Elocution

Articulating from their source in the ether, metals sustain within their sleep between planets and vowels; non-metals between zodiacal circumference and consonants.

·

Etheric Stream

The warmth process in the human being moves from head to right foot, from right foot to left hand, from left hand to right hand, from right hand to left leg, and from left leg up to the head. Streaming via the respective elemental order of earth, light, warmth, air and water, a star-like flow of the ethers guides spirit into body.

·

First Multiplication

Silence concentrates the blood's impulse toward ventricular center as centrifugal force opens neurons by sound. In every solitude, an attraction for placement; in every affinity, a multiplication. There is no *alone*: so express the rays of creation, so feels the *life* of the created.

·

Initialized By the Sense-free

The totality of feeling emanates from the Arcanum. Initialized by the sense-free, two parts are born and the inestimable generations begin.

·

Substance As Motives

As Will incarnates, motives personify substance. Embodied into substance, matter extrapolates spirit deed. Substance is the objective functioning of *atman* become impacted. The task of imaginative chemistry enters the motives within substance, appropriately *intending within* the motives themselves.

·

The Advancing Firmament

Reproduction acts through the feel for re-capitulating the first cosmic moment. All feeling enacts by initializing the sense field. Such is the cosmological legacy leading up to an actual thought.

·

The Origin of Air

Preparatory to earthly gases, the pull toward telluric center enervates from the physical conduction of light. The origin of air occurs through warmth acting *outside* itself. This is the mystery of surface, the mystery contained within surface. As such, air does what the warmth dictates.

•

The Pivot Of the Heavens

Perception is foremost a memorial to the expired, the sloughed off, the dead. The primacy of perception lives in the premonition of memory, the imagination destined. While imagination enacted the purpose of sensation, the first memory became the pivot of the heavens.

•

The Reflexive Question

Based upon memory, how does the structure of perception configure into what is capable of becoming an imagination *from* heaven?

•

The Origin of Sweetness

What is sweetness if not carbon first kissed by hydrogen, then second kissed into suspension by the nitrogen of the *astrum*?

·

The Atmosphere Throughout

The Atmosphere displays the *distillate* of sensation: the matter of hearing, sight, touch, movement *before the how* of sensing. Sensation inculcates through the portals of the body, instilling *all over* the body. How the Atmosphere emanates and reaches into the cosmos is tangible expression.

·

Sphere In Imagination

The Imagination circumscribes the conditions for body through dimensional motive. Bodily form materializes intent. Circumscribing the horizon through chemical endeavor, intent and *tonality* renew their bonds into the protean universe. As such, matter is the spirit's truest double.

·

Space-Process

As digestion animates through the paradox of cosmic beneficence, the concentrate of formative objective requires dimensional ubiquity.

•

Sentience

A clash occurs *against* sound inside the ear, a battle *against the seen* within the eye. The great effort against otherness awakens in awareness. Accordingly, as percepts distill, the transparent activates.

•

Resultant Gases

Overcoming resistance through vivifying weight, warmth reabsorbs *dimension* before contracting into air—then separately into hydrogen, nitrogen and carbon. Inspired by the heavens, air itself exhales oxygen, the necessary reagent for two-dimensional planar surface.

•

Replication

In shadow a projection is thrown of a featureless *other*; with reflection, the impression of duality is spatialized. In the world of sensation causes are twice removed. In the world of the un-sensed, effects are two-folded.

•

Preliminary Carbon

Within an organism, in order for breathing to take place fluids must lift into levity. Levity increases osmotic pressure by expressing substance out of transparence. The moment oxygen meets fluid nature, "outsides" touch the inner disposition of form. Excitedly in exhalation, a shape is born, lift occurs, a little death ensues. *Given out* through the terrestrial sphere: form is loosed, function is bound.

•

Poured Through the Elements

Light opens the cosmos, conjoining the elemental realm, its radiance below and above the senses. Heaven is discharged through the elements, their concentrations and evaporations, their alloys wedded, their tones issued. The cosmic emulsifies physical air as consciousness meets its furthermost condition in the mineral.

·

Physicality Envelope

The conditions of warmth, air and fluid amalgamate by extra-telluric sensibility. Coalesced from the wisdom of boundless dimension, boundless dimension admixes circumscribed form.

·

On Metabolism and Memory

From the depths of will, metabolism rises to meet the province of sense, cooling eventually into shape. Through the various stages of heating and rising, cooling and descending, living bodies make protein in order to maintain form. Formed, memory evaporates away from awareness into the sleeping histology of experience. As an external example of how memory accompanies the digestive mind, humid air increases the upward growth of plants while dry air decreases into awareness of the vivid.

·

On Generation

Oxidized from the life-body is the mineral-embryo. Through dreaming, the fluid-embryo is brought into air. Aroused out of sleep, the air-embryo is returned to the province of heat. This induction forms first the head, then the body. The generation of cause first forms perception, then the world.

•

Dark Earth, Hidden Attraction

Light ascends to warmth and descends into chemical action—the seed sprouts the mineral. The way to renew observation requires seeing how matter is created in the life ether, how it transmutes within tone ether, how it dies in light ether.

•

Life-Ether

The life-ether begins when solidity arises; it is characterized through carbon. The solid aggregate encountered as nature's carbon is but an end product. Through the destruction of carbon, the physical within the human being is annihilated giving rise to the spiritual. Between the lung and the kidney, liver and heart, the process from solid to liquid to air, then from warmth-ether to light-ether is enacted.

A Context For Anabolic Force

In sustaining life cyanide must be immediately destroyed in the body and excreted through the suctioning of the restorative aspect of the *mumia*. To build up the body one needs both albuminizing forces and antimonizing forces. The former are plastic substances attracted to phosphorus, the latter plastic artists binding to sulfur. Together they exhibit the balance between condensation and rarefaction.

Metabolic Satisfaction

As causal bodies re-format, substance crystallizes form. Through the nature of what satisfaction *means*, the causal bodies expand beyond image, evaporating into new protein. Making protein is incumbent upon removing past semblance while removing old protein.

Limitless Heart

The Arcanum generates the atrium of unlimited possibility. Ontologically, as the heart serves the Atmosphere, there are no metaphors for creation.

·

Lunar Pulse

Prefigured through the conduction of pulse, the efforts of the moon annunciate the flesh long in advance of the life-body.

·

Evaporation, Mineralization and Time

Elemental calcium spirals centripetally through the eons, dreamily exuding, forming the shell of creation. If otherwise contracted by primal will force, the calcium within the human skeleton would concentrate itself into the form of a mollusk. The future *was once* calcium hardening, whereas the future *will be* the skeleton dissolving. This is a crucial example of *solve* and *coagulate*.

The Nutritive Realm

Within the primacy of desire the world longs to satisfy what became its deepest hunger. What is nutrition ultimately? Digesting history to unfold dreams.

•

Warmth Toward the Periphery

Another star-like form connects right ankle (the warmth between earth and light) to the left wrist (the warmth between light and warmth); the right wrist (the warmth between air and warmth) to left ankle (the warmth between water and air); and these to the neck region (the warmth between earth and water). These five points position etheric flow and the motion of warmth from the cosmic periphery.

•

Primal Protein

Milk is a "guest drink," a potion for welcoming the newborn to earth. The role of milk wholly supports cosmic motives in their search for *corporealized* motions.

•

Satisfaction

The nature of satisfaction is commensurate to the inborn determination of what digestion *means*.

•

Etheric Context

Oxygen brings life to earth; hydrogen lifts life into the cosmos. Life-processes occur within this colloidal atmosphere, a context enabling the etheric body to "float" in matter, a dancing between warmth and form. On earth the heaviest air is carbon dioxide. How the plant infuses its etheric with this heaviness as it reaches upward is a testimonial to extra-telluric forces.

Death and Substance, Substance and Death

Formerly, air was albumin-like and alive, the body's breath-substance and nourishment. To evolve on earth, however, the death of substance is required. The airs, the gases, were all required to die in order for consciousness to arise within substance.

In the realm of substance, carbon process and the nitrogen process are closely linked. The complete protein molecule, C-O-H-N, is assailed in the metabolism; oxygen (O) and hydrogen (H) are withdrawn. What remains is cyanide, representing the death process. The combination of carbon and nitrogen *is* death.

Conference of the Elements

The realms of nature are the letters, and man is the word that is composed of these letters . . . Man's thoughts give birth to a creative force that is neither elemental nor sidereal . . . Man's thoughts create a new heaven, a new firmament, a new source of energy, from which new arts flow. When a man undertakes to create something, he establishes a new heaven as it were, and from it the work that he desires to create flows into him . . .

—Paracelsus

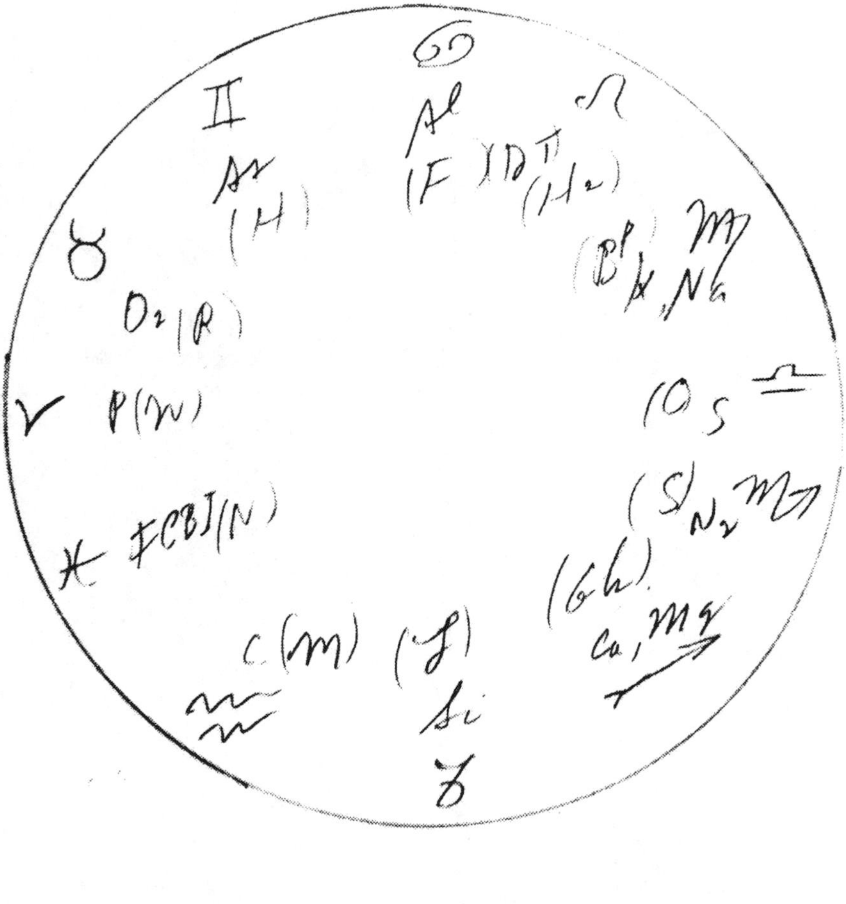

Cause and Effect

In fire substance is one. By precipitation: air, water and solids become many. Through the cooling of cosmic differentials the elements are digested toward the functional character of human nature. Effects are their causes, outwardly.

•

On the Constitution of the Elements

The Arcana's dreamt progeny, the elements, constitute from celestial ecstasy into the potency of creative elocution. On earth, elements are in fact corpses, materialized expressions of processes recalling the axiom: matter is the last step on the path of God.

•

Hydrogen

An archetypal cosmic substance, hydrogen radiates from the Central Fire, displaying the manner in which warmth reveals itself through air. With hydrogen, warmth suspends archetypal space, suspends particularization into duration. Prevalent throughout the whole of space-process, mostly warmth and combustible, this nigh insubstantial element *describes* the cosmic periphery. One could say that hydrogen *possesses* the other gases.

•

Carbon

The coursing of cosmic sympathies and telluric antipathies advance by carbon; as the former are transparent the latter grow dark. In material ablution, carbon crystallizes. Yet, by absorbing water carbon imbues life with formative force. *To grow* means to accept carbon into the organism. Accepting organic carbon permits light formation within the body; releasing carbon allows perception to meet matter. The deeper the carbon process in the body the more transformative is the distillation of life into wisdom.

•

Bath of the Astrum

The halogens: fluorine, chlorine, bromine, and iodine, summon the cognitive salts. Crystallizing near the base of the skull where the pituitary rests, cognition defines within the vault of the skull. Here, by virtue of their reactive nature, the four halogens act as a bath of the *astrum*.

•

Salt and Potassium

As *principle* flows through structure, sodium solidifies into a cube. In contrast, potassium's destiny swims toward its own demise, an imponderable exultation. While the nature of potassium aches for exhaustion, salt promotes the formative forces of the head, and wherever the head *invades* the body.

•

Soluble Salt

Least affected by the warming process, condensed away from the cosmic periphery, elemental salt offers itself into the shape of the world. The solubility of salt inverts to the congealing of imponderables. Salt risks terrestrial structure as much as light risks incarnation.

•

Silica Shapes the Firmament

On earth, the firmament weds planar impulses; warmth establishes into air by the reagent of elemental purpose. Coagulating the firmament toward solidity, silica promotes shape and connectivity throughout the fluid realm. Silica is not unlike inorganic carbon. In silica, Imagination lives as pure substance.

•

Silica and Calcium

Adhering to the laws of terrestrial space, the nature of calcium sucks away life, drying vitality into bone. Shaping life from the cosmic periphery, silica is the mother appearance, the skin of surface. The polarity between calcium and silica is such that earth and cosmos conspire physical figure and divine expression for human arrangement.

•

Sulfur and Cyanide

Sulfur and cyanide; the latter kills while the former conceives. Reproducing chemical offspring, the hysteria of sulfur prevails. In promoting human being, paradoxically cyanide is the solution.

•

Secondary Sulfur

Burning makes substance heavier, more earthly. Excepting sulfur, everything burnable was once alive, *had to* once be alive. Sulfur easily flies away from surface and from sensing while taking refuge within the history of unseen forces. Its volatile rate of change guides the metabolic into rhythm, steers the *astrum* from coalescing.

•

Nitrogen

Nitrogen expands the *astrum*'s active vehicle ubiquitously, relentlessly. Nitrogen implodes into sensible structure providing the context for *properties* and *image*. Nitrogen is seduced air taken with the animalizing body.

•

Calcium

Stabilizing the will, calcium tempts life into rest, bringing substance into alkalinity then taking it beyond to ossified ash. Carried within the collective history of excretion and sentient effort, calcium organically resonates within centripetal motion. In order to maintain the physical propensity toward figuration, calcium is continuously dissolved. As a result, the "organic" course of time *is* calcium taken into solubility.

•

Magnesium

Reigning in active light, magnesium distributes traction throughout the soluble world. In light, magnesium relaxes the overall sensory domain. Or compels it to eschew the impulses of the *astrum*. In the context of binding and loosening, magnesium enables *effusion*, the necessary yet reflexive option of time.

•

Phosphoric Ignition

Elementally impulsive, phosphorus is the bearer of available light. Combustible as it contacts air, no substance upon being burned makes as brilliant a light as phosphorus. As phosphorus burns, a thick white efflux arises. Vivid and illuminating, phosphorus promotes the astral tendency to hollow out the atmospheric air.

•

Oxygen

In darkened light, anabolic potential arouses depth of will toward embodiment. For the sense world, this is oxygen conditioning appearances, activating image and surface. The catabolic potential of oxygen melds the forces for *formative destruction* in order for will to combust into thought, for earth to inspire into center.

•

Carbonic Acid Portal

Carbon integrates matter into the terrestrial sphere, into darkness. The human being destroys carbon and forms carbonic acid. Carbonic acid is the steppingstone for light-ether, and the origin of spiritual impressions for the soul. Carbonic acid is the origin of the soul's spiritual impressions.

•

Arsenic and Symmetry

Giving objective to the etheric body, arsenic soaks up metabolic force while drying up the other metals. Arsenic de-stabilizes equilibrium while stirring the *astrum*. As absolute symmetry leads to lack of direction, arsenic leads to animal directions.

•

Aluminum Oxide

Crystalline with scattered centers, a catalyst, ductile yet resistant, visiting interiority from the *outer* depths of the cosmos: alumina: not unlike a labyrinth, a crust, reactive yet still.

•

Antimony

Condensed and rarefied, antimony by its brittle nature angles at the edges of imponderability. Guided by its structuring metabolism and image formation, the functional soul engages plasticity as it assigns boundaries. In effervescing its afterimage while embracing cosmic protein, the youthful quality of antimony *releases* life-ether.

•

The Intimacy Within Metals

Non-metals such as calcium and magnesium are of the earth, of this world. The seven archetypal metals however exist essentially as foreigners, cosmic visitors. The metals have their home within the human aura. The aura is the source of their effusion and font of their aim. As the embryonic tincture of the metals dwells throughout the earth, the character of all metals craves intimacy within human nature.

•

Metals In the Middle

The metals mediate between the zodiac and the earth. Midpoint between earth and cosmos is the human form, potent with the possibility of bringing the metals into cognitive relationship with the zodiac.

•

Lead

In metallic before-moment, conducting circulation toward the extremity of existence, lead endows spirit with a wholesome protection *from* time. Unaffected by the demands of clarity or light, lead endures as bendable darkness.

·

Tin

Fluid-like yet crystalline, formed and formlessness, tin does not readily oxidize when exposed to air. Though temperate, it easily powders when cold, yet flows when guided by warmth. As a mass tin bends, a crackling sound, the *tin cry*, can be heard due to the *twinning* force of its crystals releasing. The will within tin is highly devoted toward connectivity, inclined to conduct the most disparate aspects of formative force.

·

Iron

Sparked from heaven's lit spaces, iron breathes into the breaches of earth. Into underworld, binding, suspending, iron conducts the planetary precipitate, its metallic latticework. Steadily, iron fixates earth, refracts chemical misgivings, conditions mineral repose, all while the other metals serve the ethers.

·

Gold

As circulation extracts it force outwards from the eye, vision conducts the sun back to light. This is cosmic law. By its own centripetal axis, light manages matter's opposing tendencies. By this very luster, the source of expansion is gold.

•

Mercury

Coursing between inner world and outer realms, mercury reveals the globular as it rules the solid. Distributing intention between copper and lead, oblique connections spin into a central sphere. Refracting placement throughout the elements, mercury develops the theater of quickened ignitions, ameliorates the confusion out of chthonic dampness.

•

Copper

The *astrum*'s pull and attraction inheres in copper. The metallic intimacy within copper warms sensate feeling, exhibiting causality throughout the oxidative realm. Copper's loosening of compression is a parade of splendid undulations: as emanation, so *extraction*; as procession, so *display*.

•

Silver

Concentration is part reflection, part reproduction. Like with the moon, reflection ebbs the substance of its surface in order to relay light. In mirroring, silver sharpens skyward as it becomes rounded and burnished in heaviness. Before emanating into earth the planets mediate through the silver atmosphere. Silver refracts the metallic phantoms by way of the lunar plateau.

•

Landscape of the Metals

With silver there an orbit, with copper there is conductivity, with mercury temptation, with iron an ear, with tin a boundary, with lead admission, with gold: a throne.

•

Antimony Again

It has been noted from antiquity that the soul of human being is of the character of antimony. Antimony is diamagnetic, resisting being on earth. Paradoxically, over-distill antimony and it becomes heavy and malleable like lead. Yet, in repose, it seeks the heavens.

•

Incinerating Form, Incarnating Wisdom

Spirits of form and wisdom interweave angles of emanation, entwine for the zeal of quartz and honeycomb, embrace for the exultation of compounds.

•

The Elements Taken Through Time

The new mystery reveals how the spirits of the elements gift the self. But what is the self? Outwardly, the self emanates identity coursing the *other*. Inwardly, self is the *I* operating within a physical body. The self is the substantive entity of the elements taken cohesively through time. Above these, the self is the mystery and the magnification of splendor.

•

Tone and Protein

Through the conference of elements, the destiny of protein is the source of the earliest sense plexus. The tone-ether is required to differentiate one element from another, one destiny from another, one world from the other. Carbon, oxygen, hydrogen and carbon recapitulate the cosmos into earthly matter, into the whole meaning of the "seed."

•

Remembering the Present Tense

There are four principal colors: black, white, yellow, and red . . . Colors will then teach you how to handle fire, for they show how long and when the first, the second, and the third fire are to be made. Thence, if you are a conscientious worker, colors will teach you what to do. —John Dastin

Tools for Exploration

As shown by the forces of digestion and its and accompanying organs, the principal facts reveal that the human being *is* the consummate experiment.

•

First Concept as the Way of the Art

From the beginning onward, everything on earth *means* to constitute and develop the human being. The first concept was to create the human being. For this, substance is necessary. Sulfur for life, salt for death, with mercury weaving the original force of salt and sulfur through urges in both.

•

First Sulfur, First Phosphorus

With devotion, expectation and preservation, the Bride prepares Her wings of purity. She prepares the holy athenor to facilitate her wedding, to inspire her groom and incubate her offspring. As wisdom she cherishes the seed, the combustion, the joy. Through warmth, She lifts the horizon into the emanation of light.

•

Concentration Counters Primary Matter

Concentration opposes the tendencies of primary matter. The skeleton is heaven's terrestrial concentrate: celestial form congealed, cosmic wish embraced. Without the concentrated presence of the human being, physicality itself could not exist.

•

Overriding the Opacity In Sensing

The soul must enliven what the senses necessarily deaden. The *alkahest*, the universal solvent, resolves the dullness in sensing in order for the soul to meet the world in sense. The success of the solvent gives rise to the question: what does experience create?

•

Dysfunctional Effects Within the Subsets of Power

In the distant origins of our cosmological past the forces of the great remedy were antecedent to those of the ailment. By the forces of light and air, the principal force of creation precedes the influences of water and earth. If lost within materialized disposition however, the practitioner is but an effect of the illness.

•

Dematerializing To Assemble the Opaque

Minerals such as meteor dust, gold and cinnabar, jade, azurite, turquoise, malachite, pyrite insert their motives directly into the telluric realm. Substances such as calcite stimulate density while tourmaline's radiance expands until paradoxically vanishing. Dissolved arsenic heals, or otherwise slays. The lodestone orients from the Central Fire. Silica's translucency is itself poured resonance as it forms vision. Dematerializing the mineral, the eye activates in meeting the opaque.

•

Renovating Heaven

Like a Sun to its planets, awakened sleep addresses the metabolism's factual body. In order to renovate heaven, the circulation must gradually awaken within metabolic sleep, allowing its porous content to be a guide for inner perception and outer consciousness. Between the will of the viscera and the reality of the outer world, true sleep is a solvent of surfaces.

•

Stillness

Deeply within the skeletal system, sense activates physicality. Within bone, stillness. The relation of concentration to quiescence is through bone conduction, the osseous conduit of rhythmical potential. By the strength of *concentration*, primary matter elevates into the structural apprehension of silence.

•

Suspensions and Solutions

Intending the *Atmosphere* delivers surface to transparence. The musical or plastic sense takes desire into solution, suspending force by way of levity. Why is a solution required? Why is awareness called to it? Transparence, like music, implores the dead to impart their afterlife throughout those living. With archetypal sensitivity, the future refines by way of a solubility for which the body requires its corpse.

•

The Ambiguity of Body

Astute observation asserts that *exact* signs of death are ascertained only through the willingness of carbon relenting to ash.

•

Tenderizing Or Toughening

Poisons may contribute to tenderness as they sober the discharge of metabolism. Astringents are introduced when there's too much puff, or too little pucker.

•

Hermes Through Hypnogogia

Hermes, taking his staff, with which the eyelids of mortals close at will, and the sleeper, at will, reawakens. Seeing names, *considering* history, *feeling* the archetypes: thunder and lightening from the elemental-cosmic sphere illustrate how archaic forms discharge through the art of porosity.

·

From Melody To Matter

Beyond the physiology of sensing lies the assimilation of timbre, the accumulation of suggestion, the projection of rareness—and the circuit between them.

·

Time-Soul

The conscious soul is a time soul. The question that the Work needs to consider: how is the relationship to time disturbed or properly adjusted? Every material particle has an inner biography. Time provides, evolves and renews the context for the soul life.

·

Temporal Nexus

By virtue of the three etheric planes—sagittal-thinking, transverse-feeling and coronal-willing—future and past meet in the human diaphragm.

•

For the World

Precise knowledge of spirit has largely disappeared. To inspire soul content toward accuracy requires raising the imagination through inspiring the elements. Tangibly enlivening the inner realm as it revisions the *outside*, the hermetic motif affirms: *as outer, so in.*

•

Fear is the Adverse Chemical Music

Fear is the adverse chemical *mumia*, triggering the adverse chemical music.

•

Extraordinary Applications

The animal lives in the environment that satisfies its desires. For the Ardent the opposite is the case. Even as the seeker sheds the *mumia* of animals, he does so to ultimately distract the narrow forces of the *astrum*.

Egg of Isis

Shifting the inner horizon onto the physical ground elicits the first construction for de-sensitizing life. Desensitizing life initiates the outer horizon of evolution. This selfsame ground must be suckled with the limbs, the arches of the feet, forming a vacuum for basic levity. Lifting one's own weight into the imponderable, the body comes into light as the egg of Isis, as the font of wisdom.

•

Deconstructing the Will

Whenever the supersensible issues impulse, its body develops instinct. Activating a fulcrum of directed desire, the future is pulled into the present. Here, the seed force of will wrestles itself into imagination. As the not-yet materialized nature of creation specifies the conditions for its presence, the dream of inverted resolve *enacts* the here and now. Comprehending this re-members the present tense.

•

Creative Elimination

Teeming with impulses from the creative lineage of the Firmament, the Art meets the reality of feces. About excrement, the work must reveal that none but *those* capable of creation could separate corporeality from chaos in order to digest the fruits of existence. Accordingly, by one's own feces the way to creation is shown.

•

Causality

Seeing effects as set between two determinations reclaims the causal context while quickening the effect's outpour. Potentized in the womb of the circulatory chambers, the Microcosm rides all measures high and low.

•

Carefully Salted, Ready to Go

Salt is form. Inspired salt permeates the nerve pole and wherever the head forces "invade" the body. Directing the respiration toward salt releases enchantments, freeing misshapen dispositions of the body and soul. With the breath salted, the will gathers the metabolism, aiding individualized form. With salted breath, the self may approach the *I* from the *outside* without this killing the *self.*

·

By A Shrunken Power

There are certain forces far exceeding the worst horrors, destroying that which has not yet been conceived. Their charm grows into a homunculus, eventually becoming a universal creature enchanted *into* disinterest for bodily form.

·

Big Deep

In winter, those ardent store their thoughts below ground, into the depths of earth. Doing so, they obtain the favors of the earth's truest spirit, the planet's inner awakened clarity.

·

Because, This

Soul meets sensation through embodied sense recapitulating world substance. Ever since causation was arrested from creation, the need to unravel matter's depths has mistakenly been considered the way *into* the world.

•

Combining and Unraveling

Differing in high summer or midwinter, combining the time tenses orchestrates the *Archeus*. Reviewing time backwards apprehends the mellifluous coursing of the higher self.

•

Awakened Presence

Agrippa von Nettesheim maintained that one can be so asleep as to be *present* to divine nature. This astute observation refers to the *thanos melete*, the sweet death of awakened possibility. In this sleep what is typically obliterated by sense-laden material-bound consciousness surfaces as soul perceiving the spirit's presence.

·

Atmospheric Adjustment

The Ardent releases his ethers from suppositional understanding. His work will at times require adjusting the sky in order to see the manner in which essence is married to transparence.

·

As If the World Already Ended

By the rhythmical power of *moral* carbon the conditions for new world evolution funnel into the formative ethers. Here, the body of liberated intent displays the active Atmosphere.

·

A Brief Yet Far-reaching Repertory

Two of the cosmos' chief ingredients are carbon and hydrogen. Proteins require the addition of hydrogen and nitrogen. For establishing the whole of the planetary disposition however, phosphorus and sulfur must be added.

·

Yearning For the Cosmic Fulcrum

Consider the work as engaging wisdom through terrestrial devotion.
Observe as the Bride intends her shape around the cosmic fulcrum.

·

Weight Reassembled

By means of normative chemistry, elements fall by the weight of thought
as the world is further misguided. Forced pressure decays the atmosphere;
forced visibility bruises the heart. Triumphant yet shivering, the elements
radiate from their earthly center into the core of porous intent. Into
the *Atmosphere* the new chemical urge enters elemental fortitude, grows
flushed through the senses, tones heaviness into ardor, rectifies matter by
lifting its weight.

·

Unwrapping the Mummification

Great danger lies in the belief that our species is left to its own devices. An even greater danger lies in believing that we are *not* left to ourselves. Unwrapping the mummification wrought by abstractions, arrogance and fear, transmutations are chosen that are pivotal for changing the turbid into the intelligible, and the shaken into the steadied. Drawing spirit into the inert while elevating the inert into spirit requires the fixative of attention, the crucible of potent causation. By this active devotion there is no divorcing spirit from stone. This liberates transparence with the whole of its light.

•

Warmth Reconsidered

Since heat phenomena first *appears* as space phenomena, normative chemistry is constrained to think of heat as spatial, mimicking concepts of solids. For an adequate understanding of warmth, the thinking must rise through the physics of space into non-spatial relations. The Work must be attentive to the polarity between heat and pressure. Pressure does what heat is supposed to do, but does not penetrate like heat, which interpenetrates everything. Warmth is a higher substance-concept predicated on will activity; to understand warmth means to distinguish how it behaves within ourselves.

•

Twice Sweetened Melody

In wintry season the beehive inclines cosmic momentum inward. In spring, the hive hums its devotion, announcing the ascendancy of metabolism seeking sweetness. Readying to offer their toil to the Queen of Everything, the bees seek nectar in their unyielding demonstration of love.

•

The Qualities of Time

Inspired, vision coagulates into telluric formation. Deep within the earth, the waxing moon increases the movement of fluids. Waning, the lunar influence convenes solution to stillness. By these, the world imbues with the qualities of time.

•

The Precipitate

As the philosopher Raymond Lully disclosed: the Virgin is the Arcanum of the Art. She is the force that provokes and instigates. Through her the precipitate is offered though not simply given away.

·

The Gradual Dispersion

Circulation is the vehicle for cosmic inversion. Imponderably paused, blood is the audacity of primal heat.

·

The Given-over

Regarding substance: as the flow of blood *pauses* before disappearing into the cosmos, fire generates new forms by destroying blood, makes new blood by destroying old forms.

·

The Charm Within the Sensorium

Attempting to visit the interior, the embryonic *disposition* first meets the work mentally as well as spatially; here, the brain mirrors the processes of mental imagery and thought. Casting off the dross after absorbing the image, this charm within the *sensorium* gives way to the condition of ardor, heat, *tapas,* where causality is apprehended within the viscera. In this ripening process the mood itself increases specific faculties and discernments for maturing the work. Here, the "blossoming of time" dreams nitrogen's imagery *backwards*, willing the time-tenses into the *Potent Body*.

•

The Art of Darkness

Consciousness elicits ideational malabsorption whenever thoughts disintegrate or become obstructively random. The art of darkness distinguishes how putrefied thoughts in fact exist within the macabre degenerations of feces, undigested.

•

The Dead Talking

For all intents, by the path of porosity those who seek metamorphosis already lead the life of the dead. They drink the crystalline *pharmakon* while enjoying the heavenly psychosis.

•

Center and Periphery

While the head is *here*, the limbs radiate from cosmic center; the limbs are a consequence of *thereness*. Regarding the limbs, the periphery is their center. As for the head, here the cosmos reaches its furthest point. The center of the head is the periphery for the cosmos.

•

Pushing and Pulling

In and out, pushing and pulling: when conceived of as rarefaction throughout the motions of intercourse, this means to set up a vacuum.

•

Longing Upon the Starry Mist

By their own nature, poisons compliment creation. Dreaming the toxicity, releasing the venom, this mirrors the nature of the heavenly.

•

Portrait of Time As It's Coming To Be

Inside perception weave conditions of particularization, the qualities of time, moods and hues of the unconscious. The outward force of the Arcanum diffuses as creation withstands the majesty of atmospheric darkness. Time instills within the shadows cast by angels.

•

Poisoned By the Same Forces

While enemies are born through compounded iron, friends are poisoned by similar forces.

•

Philosophic Mercury

With its caduceus-like neck braided around an alembic of clear intent, the swan is the hermetic symbol of philosophic mercury. At home on earth, in water or in the air, the swan represents the conscious encounter with life-ether. It is unbothered by sun or ice, indifferent to harsh conditions; it is a being whose mutability meets nearly all circumstance. With its beautifully rounded body upon which rests an extended phallic neck, the swan's mystical-erotic connotations illustrate the wedded satisfaction of desires. Looking up to the summer night's constellation of Cygnus, the Swan, its *signature* impresses the alchemical objective regarding the illuminating of primal matter by pure intent.

•

On the Motives of the Spleen

Within animated warmth blood clarifies circulatory motives. The spleen, Saturn's microcosmic analog, may undergo a *numinous* release, a premonition of the new Atmosphere through the blood's willingness to die into new form. In order for the general world porosity to imbibe its dispersion, the spleen upholds this objectivity.

•

The Future In Sensing

Embryology reveals psychology: the head contracts for earthly experience, the body expands for heavenly experience. Looking to the heavens is looking into the past, the history of cosmic being. Reconciling with the emanations from the stars, one finds the stars exist in the present tense only here on earth. On earth alone one finds the present tense. For the future, the work needs to develop *manas, buddhi, atman* through feeling, balance, movement.

•

Psychoemblemata and the Alchemical Venture

Though images and color immediately speak to the modern psyche, precious little attention is given to the inner life of imagery itself, how it weaves its surface between imagination and perceptual vision, how it births through the forces of imagination, informing soul not merely as picture or metaphor but as reality. For imagery to yield fresh perception, entering the *being* of color is basic for educating the soul. In meeting *blue* one meets light seen through darkness; blue is a *fact* of the sky, the active light of heaven meeting the boundary of night. As its luster denotes active sense function, blue's soul is form-giving, coagulating the divine realm for the senses and cognition, appropriating how perception structures imagery. In contrast, one meets *red* as ethereal darkness obscuring light. Red is chiefly earthly and visceral, the living metabolic luster of life. Through iron's connection with blood, through blood's association with elemental fire, through obscuring light, red appears as the oxidizing inclination of the metals and the inflammatory tendencies of sulfur and carbon. Through the history of alchemical and astrological imagery examples abound illustrating color and form displaying these kinds of intrinsic qualities; symbol and soul are united, living as the fabric of reality in the deeper imagination when color is understood in the breath and feeling of soul. Admixing blue and red the raiment of royal violet is born, a conjunction of the neurological and biological, an expression of forces marrying one another. As the continuum of spirit and substance lives in the language of World Soul, Imagination works actual experience through the *body* of psyche.

Speaking the soul's language, alchemical aim wishes to uncover the mysteries inherent in spirit and matter. As the Ardent extracts the *massa confusa* out from the aspirations of the psyche, accurate emblems encountered within his soul create clearer imagery of what is needed to further the work. Though a history of misguided examples abound, the Ardent is concerned with fructifying nature's motives and his own by envisioning the future through purified intent. Within this wish, *ensouled* relation to color, sense, form and matter engages the enormity of cosmic yearning.

•

Placing Suspensions in Solution

Whatever finds itself directed toward transparence is not won over by facts, but by purpose. These solutions further the causes of the Unknown.

•

Primary Form and Nuptial Intent

The egg carries the imaginations from blood, sperm the images of form. By the forces of the moon the body exists as seed, its urges dream within light. Light mixed with the earthly principle directly confuses creation. From confusion onwards, human form exists in the elements, requiring a marriage between heaven and earth.

•

Love and Destruction

Destroying the *matrix* brings creation into the realm of earth. Lovingly destroying ourselves sets our human form into the stars. Constitutive of the human being, death is the bodily devotion between Arcanum and Atmosphere.

•

The First Concept, Emanating

The first concept was to create the human being. Everything on earth *was* and *is meant to* constitute and develop the human being.

The intersecting spirits of will and wisdom provide the form where the dream of silica begins. The triangle of heaven meets itself anew when meeting itself upside down.

The metals sustain their individuality between planets and vowels; the non-metals between the zodiac and consonants.

Behind the zodiac is another world and the Cosmic Ram turns to gaze upon it. The Virgin anticipates *through* it. The Serpent Bearer, the cosmic Artifex, has both the celestial equator and the ecliptic passing through him.

Burning substance makes it heavier, more earthly. Everything burnable was once alive. Yet, burning sulfur is the exception to generating heaviness. Alchemically, sulfur represents life, salt death. Mercury leads into and through both, breathing.

As the two halves of the chemical *mumia* transpire into one, the *astrum* quickens.

Iron is needed to dominate the *astrum*; sulfur and oxygen to uplift cyanides. Arising out of the amphora, the serpent and its venom are subdued by the Art. With uncorrupted intent, both inner and outer poisons are overcome.

The philosophic stone is the universal remedy and antidote. Within the appropriate form its wisdom is employed when there is need to eliminate nitrogen from the organism.

With devotion, expectation and preservation, the Bride prepares for her Groom, her nuptials and her offspring. Her wisdom cherishes the seed while her wings display her purity. As she carries her warmth, She guides the emanations of light. Painful in this splendor: love and carbon, carbon love, planet love. Through nuptials, tone marries iron to oxygen.

The *human* form extends the light within the head by the warmth throughout the viscera. Through elongating the skull, the heart reaches for infinity by the force of the limbs.

The warmth within the Arcanum is the light within the Art. Where is it? Everywhere. What does it contain? Everything. To lovingly destroy the matrix buries the Work into earth. To lovingly destroy the soul sets the *self* into the stars. From this the Atmosphere assembles through the firmament's suction, a new sugar.

•

Additive Invisibility and
Chemical Intent

Every disease is a musical problem. Every cure, a musical solution. —Novalis

High Heat

Combustion develops a heat beyond any scorching fire. Roasting once, distilling twice, Achamoth, Ophis, Hermes Thrice!

•

Heat Evolving

As a fulcrum between enchantment and resistance, the Microcosm guides heat into reflection, reflection into separation, separation into body. The body evokes, the psyche involves. By inner firmament, heat evolves.

•

Three Mirror Reflex

Deepening incarnation requires three mirrors: the reflecting mirror of tactile imagination; the participating mirror of cosmic feeling; the projecting mirror of world resolve.

•

Time-based Chemistry

Normative chemistry utilizes aborted impulses stripped from a spiritual connectivity to world becoming. Under this kind of material-based influence, conditions for apprehending the future grow evermore handicapped, weaker by the moment. With time-based chemistry the landscape of the metals means to fructify. In suctioning the present from the future, the past is brought into solution.

•

Time-Body

Coaxing the *ouroboros* out of his circle, the body uncoils, accessing working *through* time. *Into* their hub of sensation, the refracted senses contribute to unfurling the causal Atmosphere. Into resurrected air, light disperses active being from recollected warmth. By *cognizing* light, thought serves the Atmospheric *display*. From this, light sees itself in *seeing*, without beginning or end.

•

Transubstantiation

In transubstantiation the accidents through time remain the same while the substance itself changes.

·

Two Aspects of Being Burnable

Within its potential, physical substance burns due to its readiness to become ash. Substance is burnable due to the innate tendency of its own inner fire to reach for heaven.

·

Warmth, Penetration and New Warmth

Every interior becomes an exterior whenever it cannot produce its own heat. To comprehend heat, attention must press forward into *reversed space*: space behaving negatively within counter-image. The interior warmth of Imagination penetrates surface exteriority, porously offering inner gesture into outer claim. All penetration arises from the Central Fire's ability to decompress the world backwards.

·

The Will to Matter

Separating and magnifying: both stir matter. *Separation* quickens substance out of latency; *magnification* extends substance into force. This is Will *becoming*.

•

A Corrective for Bodily Betrayals

Inimical forces enter the Art, illusions posing as truth. The way through confusion requires the life-body to sustain matter, to reflect formal cause, emanate causal appearance. This locates motive within substance, forces as intent. As life gathers light, there are betrayals of the ether for which induced purges often yield brilliant results.

•

A Sulfuret of Silver

There are some oils that contain considerable sulfur such as those of mustard, asafetida and allium. Placed in one of these oils silver quickly darkens due to its *uniting* with the sulfur. Throughout catabolic transudation, as sulfur overcomes silver's reflective disposition, a sulfuret is produced. Throughout transmutation, sulfur provides the agency for renewed ebullience.

•

Above and Below

For the over-soul, the active agent requires concentrating the cosmic periphery. Intending harmonic motion above knowing and below sleep, the *concentrate* activates in the sublimated current of undertones.

•

Archetypal Fluids

As no other among metals, mercury exists naturally as a fluid. Throughout the whole of the firmament of self, blood courses deliberately as the liquid organ.

•

Awareness

The inverse within matter coagulates heat, coalesces light, meets surface. By the rhythm of breath and blood, by sense-outpour meeting the fingerprints of the soul, awareness *de-physicalizes* the mineral, "takes up" through the furthest emanation of celestial influence. Through de-physicalization, color breathes through perceptual space. Here, the will may be appointed toward conditioning matter.

•

Blood and Nerve

Against the movement of blood, awareness lives in direct relationship to the *other*. Through nerve, the potential for consciousness is emptiness.

•

By Way of Laterality

Those right-handed stir in a clockwise direction; those left-handed, in a counter-clockwise motion. This portrayal of the ether body illustrates the centrifugal impulse of metabolism as well as the centripetal tendencies from sensation.

•

Calcination

Within ideation is the blossoming of dreamt will. Within dreamt will, the primary constitution of the physical body regenerating warmth. From Saturn's original heat, light into pure light is delivered by *calcination*. Earth-warmth into assembled-warmth initiates white through the ultimate impulse for the Vulcan condition.

•

Catalytic Reflex

Structuring the outer, the catalytic reflex of nerve metabolizes surface into exteriority. For chemical intent to activate the under-conscious, the will reflex permits substance to dissolve into time as time admits the moment into eternity.

•

Causality

Ibn' Arabi noted that every cause is the effect of its own effect. A full moon favors the increase of etheric substance, a new moon its disappearance. Chemically, every effect takes on the power of its causal bodies, building up or tearing down the original power. Paradoxically in the world of effects, if a power harbors pathological potential, the cause putrefies. If nurturing an enlightened power, the cause fructifies.

●

The Chemical Divorce

The *illiaster* yearns into what life alone cannot attain. By autonomic charge, *misformations* unleash obsession, unraveling into discontent. Through magnifying crucial partings, nuptials are disclosed.

●

Chemical Basics

Normative chemistry addresses the telluric realm, the realm that suffers its being and existence through weight and pressure in order to bring about intent. Alchemically, weightlessness with its extra-telluric and interstitial force is employed to magnify intent. *Magnification* uses low pressure and low heat whose analogs are chewing and understanding.

●

Darkness and Light

As the conduit for light-ether, darkness' cosmic opacity cradles the womb of expectancy, the font of the Atmosphere. The universally unfathomable condition is the substantive mirror of matter itself growing excited, anticipating revelation.

•

Sulfur Year

The time of the year can be divided in four sulfur periods: autumn is when the alchemical sulfur relates to the child; winter when the alchemical sulfur relates to the adolescent; spring when the alchemical sulfur relates to the adult, and high summer is when the alchemic sulfur relates to the aged.

•

Dematerializing the Mineral

Substances such as calcite stimulate density while those such as tourmaline expand until they vanish. Among others, meteoric iron and pyrite display distinct motives from the cosmic realm, while the flow of lava lifts the mineral out from the Central Fire. Silica's translucency pours resonance as its form meets vision. Dematerializing the mineral within the senses, sensation functions by meeting the impenetrable.

Destiny and Hydrogen

Hydrogen is capable of being burned, producing water after ignited. Proteins are generally sulfurous, quick to decay without some opposing anabolic pull. While the ovum is mostly protein, semen is full of hydrogen. As semen discharges toward its destination, the egg evaporates, transmuting hydrogen into new destiny.

•

Devotion Multiplies Through Lead

When chemical intent reaches into Saturn's sphere, lead transmutes into freshened mercury. To liberate the metals in the crucible of the *astrum*, mercury is obliged to multiply through lead, take on the luster of yellow Sun then summarize into red as devotion instills into matter.

•

Dying Out Of Self

Though born out of the mother matrix, substance resists fixating into matter. Projecting the effects of light, the battle between substance and matter tempers soul-shape into finding specific placement between them. While substance evaporates out of the world-placenta, matter exalts out of dimension into spirit.

•

Evaporated Thought, Metabolic Relief

Within the universal solvent, life-ether distils out actualized tone through the severance of sound. In this crucible of the *unheard*, density is inflamed, combusted, resolving amplitude, modulating pitch. Unclouded by material fixation, the metabolism readies to meet the harmonic potential of the *Potent Body*.

•

Universal Antidote

Appropriately enlisted for eliminating nitrogen, the *lapis* acts as the remedy for *restating* the forces of carbon, igniting the joy of affection, affirming the gift of the self to the other.

•

From Metallic Intent to High Sensitivity

The planetary metals concentrate through inherited lunar fixation. The cosmos' own sensibility sculpts the metallic inversion of will. The heaviest gases breed from negative predication. Weightless, the philosophic stone is the organ of highest sensitivity.

•

From Iliaster to Reflection

When phosphorus rules the disposition, dispossessed matter stirs appearance. In the *mumia* phosphoric activity is observable; see the *iliaster* reflected throughout the discharge. Breathe the *iliaster* into vapor to illustrate those substances capable of reflection.

•

From Reflection to Iliaster

The limitation of the *astrum* is found throughout its shadows. Directed onwards, lunar resolve reflects light, its shadow force refracting. Though sensitive to light, reflection is numb to warmth. Refraction is centrifugal, reflection centripetal. With active imagination, nitrogen reflects the cock, carefully revealing the vulva.

·

Homeostasis

The viscera express heat into the overall circulation. The blood lives in opposition to the corpuscle. By sheer effort, the fluid element orients directly out of will. Stilling vitality into nodes of apprehension, each organ seeks to modulate periphery and center.

·

Ouroboros

To further the operant *Archeus*, the Ardent involutes experience, taking *sensing* to meet the root of the self. Meeting the ether-body of his youth, the Ardent bites his own tail, recharging the power of devotion.

•

Housing the Signatures

The microcosm amalgamates etheric activity within gestures of life-body. Gestures of the functional soul display their figurative distillation into chemical copy. Planetary-wise, the *signatures* lead the imagination to the art of placement.

•

Mumia

The *mumia* is the vehicle through which the Will acts, effectuating benefit or harm. The *mumia* contains characteristics of whichever being sustains the vital force of another; it is closely connected with the bloodstream. As a result, any substance absorbed into the blood makes a direct connection between the *mumia* receiving the substance and the *mumia* from whatever it was taken. Through the *mumia* shame and fear reproduce themselves as blushing and paleness; unexpected joy may cure a disease, sudden terror may result in death. Envy and hatred may generate morbid imaginations resulting in illness. Notably, the *mumia* may be guided by the power of the *imagination*, which, when rightly fathomed, is a tremendous force able to create genuine images in the ether, giving consciousness to those noumenal forms.

●

Infused to Aid the Astrum

Distilled by the dreamt elixir of the chemical *mumia*, the life-body is the first light touched by the cosmic *astrum*. As the infusion directs from the greater firmament toward the digestive soul, the vitality is charged with prescient fortitude, the atmospheric protein condenses into the self.

●

Lemniscate Of the Metallic Aura

The six metals serve the etheric body, which is their home. The Work can dynamically address the lead human being, the tin human being, the gold, mercury, copper and the silver human being. Only iron is present as an unpotentized metal in the blood; it is the bridge between the etheric body and the physical.

●

Lunar Faculty

The moon has the capacity to pull out the *Archeus*, pull out the forces from the formative body. If the moon is rightly directed, the will can be guided into the body as an available power for imaging formative force.

•

Life-ether

Projecting *un-thought* creation, the chemical cross extends its boundary through dimensions, reaches through the life-ether as the principal *arrangement*.

•

Light To Gold

Instilling the Arcanum from earthly effects, the cosmos conducts structurally through the elemental realm. Here, substance is masked as the senses construct the world in its material relationship. On the other hand, within the senses, the nature of substance may be uncovered beyond the physical, as light is comprehended by truly envisioning gold.

·

Love, Fate and Carbon

By rhythmic destiny the cosmic *ouroboros* sheds universal surface, the galactic skin. For the metabolism, the celestial molt re-births carbon. By this, the blood may know sweetness; and by this, it knows it not.

·

Making New Salt

Space ventures gesture into shape, draws form by renovating surface. As the periphery orients to center, the circle triangulates. As the center sleeps, the cube evaporates. This creates salt.

·

Making New Substance (Redux)

Permeated, expanded with devotion, the Art captures the bull by the tail, births two birds from one stone, arrives early for its own wedding. The mercury-force pulls the cloak over fear, dives around belief, refreshes by re-aligning sight. Unlike those who argue from opinions, the Art aspires to a release the world from opinions.

Oxidation begets heaviness. From a source traced to sacrifice, metabolic sweat delivers the gift for levity, levity for accessing transparence. When perception is wedded to extraction, phenomena yield cause. Sensible love and active love: the first is coagulated and bloody, the other is porous and dry.

Faith develops how the future meets necessity. By the course of faith, substance is not purified just any way: the mercurial dimension elicits appearance and invention, disappearance and demise. As the Art touches matter, Hermes is met not once but twice.

Burying oneself beneath the earth, the inner light may apprehend the origins of dreams and obtain the favors of the cosmos. Encountering surface: a corpse is a corpse—until revived and arisen.

•

Materia Prima

Out of the abyss heaven is cast forth, the *materia prima* forecasting the completion of man. Hidden in the human being are both abyss and heaven. Revealed in the work is the redemption of the particle through attaining the whole.

•

Motives As Substance

Inimical to heightened awareness, certain putrefactions and retardations take cover within the *astrum*. Regardless, throughout the expansion into *consciousness soul*, sublimation decays the hidden into the renewed causal substrate.

•

Nothingness Structuring the World

There is an ontological gap, a space, where cosmic sympathies and antipathies meet. This synaptic space frees into spirit. To achieve world-making, self ignites this abyss into the structure of the world.

•

Nutritive Soul

Aroused by projective hunger, life-ether enlivens from warmth-substance, offering matter into the new Atmosphere. Individuation digests the *prima materia* into the sphere of planetary resolution—satisfaction through dissolution.

•

On Dissolution

Dissolution supports the coagulative condition, sacrificing spirit into mineral. For created substance, the uncreated is its skin. In view of this, the world was never invented.

•

Particularized Light, Particularized Warmth

The imponderables of thinking and digestion are particularized light and particularized warmth. Thought emanates the cosmic exterior; digestion carries forth the depths of cosmic interior. Through the body of Saturn, the soul's rhythmical Sun, the bodily-formative Moon: Conducting outward through the infinitesimal moment, particularized light, particularized warmth suffer measure, number and weight.

•

Pausing the Will

The rhythmic potential between transparence and Atmosphere enables the projection for pausing the will, etching transparence, modulating *character*. Character exhibits its own *cauda pavonis,* displaying radiance while awakening in destiny.

•

Gathered Together From the Seed of Hermes

Seeing quality, *hearing* causes, *touching* the archetypes: even without mineral substance these functional "organs" are akin to lungs, kidneys and bowels. As with the surface tension of the *sensorium* outside, so the mystery within unveils. The *astrum* is the source for apprehending the foundation towards a deeper understanding of the senses: portals to the twelve-fold character of the cosmos. At the core of the *astrum* is the human soul-spirit by way of thinking, feeling and will. To visit the interior, the distillate of the inner realm enlivens. To sense with inner illumination radiates the seed of Hermes. Acting from this power is walking with the gods.

•

Formative Gold

Chemical resolve lifts image out from substance. From the *carbonate of planets* breathes out a six-sided luster, darkness into form. Evaporating into light, form reflects the forces needed for the heart.

·

Reflexivity and Love

By releasing cosmic memory into the present tense, love rejoins the particulate soul to the Beginning. Uplifting creation's weight is in fact love.

·

Surface and Surfactant

In the sleep of relationship, dimension presents surface through gestures of dormancy. Chemical conscience is a surfactant awakened *as* time, made supersensible. Awakened sleep entices surfaces to "disappear."

·

Chemical Wedding

Like the full moon, the mind's *substance* reflects the Atmosphere. Like the new moon, thinking substance reflects emptiness. As the brain mirrors processes of mental imagery and conceptualization, thinking activates the dynamics of center and periphery. Freeing substance out of thinking substance, the distillate becomes mineral, the amalgam chemical.

•

World Ending

In world-becoming the cosmos divides and delineates. Celestial decay and terrestrial assimilation both bear this physical burden. Insides and outsides fleetingly transfix while their excreta are shadows cast off. Within material digestion the world effectively ends. All relationship requires absorption.

•

Facsimile of the Present Tense

Projection establishes essence. *Then*, *now*, and *when* resonate into one another, coalescing the sound the etheric requires in order to be apprehended as time. Between the soul and its image in spirit is the realm of prepared facsimile, inventing the present tense.

•

The Inverted Present

The *lapis* in Atwood's *A Suggestive Inquiry* is regarded as "being sublimed at first, it is called a serpent, dragon, or green lion, on account of its strength and crude vitality, which putrefying, becomes a stronger poison, and their venomous toad; which afterwards appearing calcined by its proper fire, is called magnesia and lead of the wise."

Then again, upon closer examination, courting warmth while erasing the flesh *salinates* the story of sulfur. With repetition and resolve, the sense-bath offers itself to conjugal vision.

•

The Green Snake and Exquisite Intent

Dominating the *astrum* requires schooling iron; in the Work sulfur and oxygen are needed to uplift cyanides. Deep within the blood, arising out of the abyss, desire is trained by the faculties of venom. With uncorrupted intent, poisons are attenuated into their proper destiny.

•

Preservation and Occluded Invisibility

Compounds perish by lawful corrosion or preserve by lawful anabolism. Add the sphere to the cube to apprehend the mutability of salt. Afterwards, add the tetrahedron, making the whole of the image disappear.

.

Reflective Capacity

The Art requires the totality of body, soul and spirit. Whole, the Ardent is capable of creating a mirror *for* the face of the cosmos.

.

Radiance, Heaviness and Understanding

Radiance amends might and heaviness; heaviness modifies through radiance and light. Left on their own, each rules the other by confusion, each ruins the other by contempt.

.

Remembering Inner Geometry

Inscribed within the layers of the viscera, Inspiration eternally *streams* toward the self. Through this flow, inner intent surfaces the condition for *remembrance.* Through meeting the internal periphery, the inner geometry is revealed.

•

Second Force

Though the effects of substance foment through the space-process, essence rests in biomorphic time, acoustic space. The force of substance must be continuously re-membered as it is relentlessly forgotten: Hermes breathing through soul. This paradox radiates the future, respiring between salt and space, sulfur and transformation. Evolving within the forces of sleep, the future resists the space-process, entering the Atmosphere through inner music, inner geometry, inner grammar.

•

Self-Correction Through Bone

Inspiration into the chemical-tone-ether develops the bony skeleton. And Imagination redeems the notion that the world lives *in* time.

Sense Existence As the World

The senses are constituted for freeing creation in inverse proportion to the display of the body. The world exists as the exteriority of senses reflected into display.

•

Solve and Coagula

The powers of metamorphosis are engaged by placing the soluble into the coagulated, the contracted into the porous. The eagle moves to bind, the lion moves by loosening. Salt and sulfur each seek their own directive.

•

Sublimating Sulfur

Ash from vegetal sources contains a certain quantity of silica. Silica may be employed to sublimate the ebullience of sulfur. Correctly utilizing silica, the consonance in substance congeals the qualitative spirit by expanding the quantity of lifelessness.

•

Subtracting Time, Adding Time

Salt arrests disintegration through mineral repose. While salt dominates the catabolic, sulfur leads the anabolic. Combing hair releases sulfur into space; urinating streams sulfur to earth. Sulfur circulates warmth clockwise while assisting disintegration. In putrefaction, corrosive digestion requires oxidizing, acidifying and separation. These processes radiate sulfur yet can emulate salt. By contracting sulfur's radiance into salted toil, the elements reenter an etheric condition: time, where they are motivated by way of mercury.

•

Iron Into Warmth

Whenever chaos arises in the body, an attempt is made to build a new ear. Listen for its adverse chemical noise. The task of listening is to take iron over into the warmth-ether, into the *will* via the ear.

·

Suspending the Fallen Mercury

The tension within the individualized *mumia* is the interplay between attitude and aptitude. By suspending the fallen mercury, the point of tension continuously redefines whatever needs to be excreted.

·

The Chemical Mumia

As the two halves of the chemical *mumia* transpire into one, the *astrum* quickens, the Arcanum waits. The soul gathers the force for encountering the corpse it helped create.

·

The Green Lion

In physical death the life-ether blossoms into the marrow of transparence. Its after-dew is a loveliness through which cosmic substance itself quickens. *Anamorphizing* substance, the Green Lion devours the Sun, its rhythmical fixative. Its circulation spirals towards the precipitated dew, erasing exteriors as it proceeds to visit the interior. Such is vitriol.

•

The Eye's Elixir

Heating a ladleful of soft lead or beeswax atop a flame gradually dissolves the mass into a fluid state. The liquefied substance when quickly poured into a vessel of cool water congeals. Observing the resultant form unveils circulatory motives: the coagulated shape reveals the *astrum* conducting an imagination for solubility, the Sun as the eye's elixir.

•

The Transparent Brings to Body

Hydrogen penetrates the airs around all surfaces; nitrogen coalesces the breath of light; oxygen initiates movement while carbon is the heart of darkness. Transparence reveals the ratio of the archetypal gasses, bringing them to their source in the body.

•

The Universal Menstruum

The task of the *menstruum* is to renew the capacities of the world womb. In the single-chambered heart, the alembic light cultivates the *lapis*. This reflexive circulation effectively resists its own weight, circulating brain and womb as two-moon-ed.

•

The Art of Invisibility

Distilling the core of formative force, Imagination schools the soul's understanding. Through mercurial salt, the ethers bind. The power of the *lapis* utilizes the art of invisibility.

•

Placing and Palpating the Attention

Sleep develops sweetness through the resonances from Venus and Moon. Wakefulness increases through the savor of the outer planets: Mars, Jupiter and Saturn. Released by the anatomical Arcanum, the inner planets oppose noxious tendencies that destroy the will, while the outer planets rectify unfocused attention by clarifying imagery. Placing the attention, concentration pivots from the iron-phantom, palpates the reflectivity of silver, embrocates by the nurture of the Sun. This grows insight.

·

Visit the Interior

Meeting causality visits the questions of decay and strife. For this, light carefully hollows out vitality to properly configure the *astrum*. Inspiration next suctions in cosmic force through enlightened in-breath as metabolism meets the forces of youth, vitality and childhood. Through this, the Ardent revisits the interior of his own earth by visiting the interiority of the whole of matter's past. The inmost elixir is assembled as: *Visita Interiora Terrae Rectificando Invenies Occultum Lapidem.*

·

A Solvent of Surfaces

The Ardent can fully occupy his own shape in awakened sleep. This true sleep is a solvent of surfaces. Asleep, intent attains the perfect sphere.

·

Disassembly to Transparence

Disassembled through porosity, the head evaporates by the laws of karma, the body dissolves by supra-sensory ether, the *nigredo* separates and sorts. By repetition working through the raven's head, an ash of potent mercury activates putrefaction. Sense to surface echoes by relaxing sense from solids.

•

Comprehending the Imponderable

Comprehending the *remedy* requires pulling into space the null point within compression, extracting the power of the *Archeus* within digestion.

•

The Bath of Radiance

The present tense breathes the Atmosphere as love marries carbon. Toward the *Potent Body* by the bath of radiance, the swimming swan solves a wing afore; the black swan, the hinge of heaven.

•

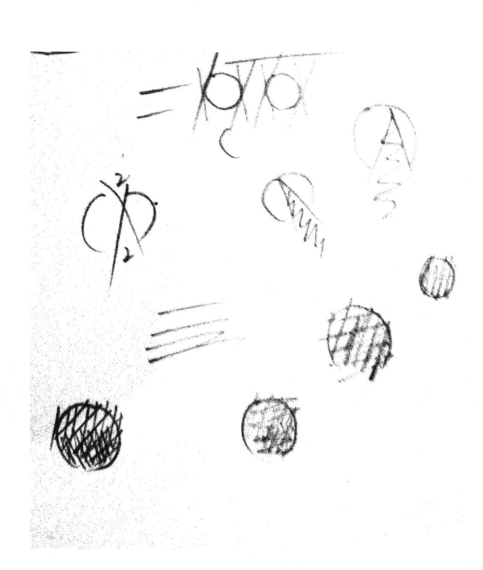

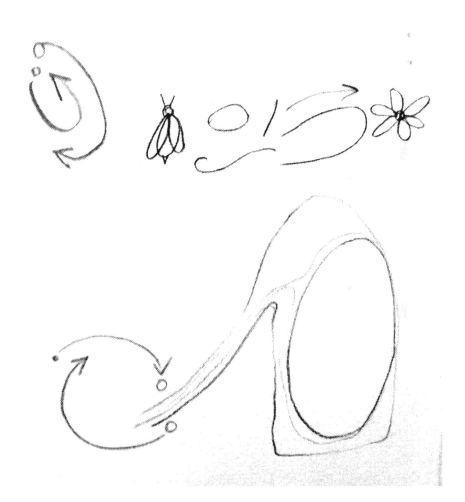

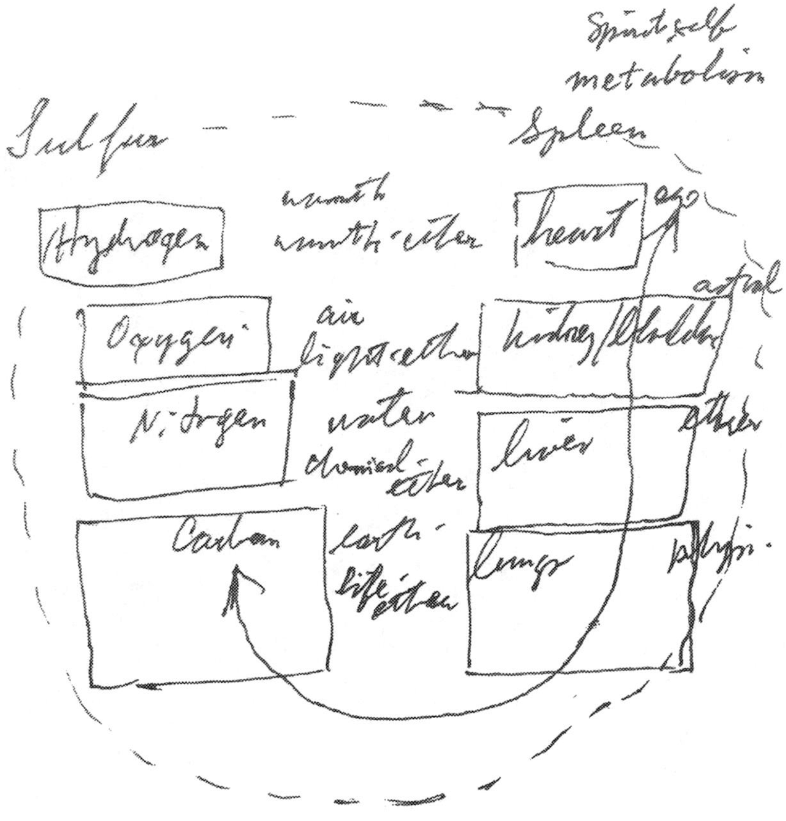
Spirit self
metabolism
Sulfur
Spleen
Hydrogen
warmth
warmth-ether
heart
ego
astral
Oxygen
air
light-ether
kidney/bladder
Nitrogen
water
chemical-ether
liver
etheric
Carbon
earth
life-ether
lungs

Projections and Nuptial Chamber

First we bring together then we putrefy; we break down what has been putrefied; we purify the divided; we unite the purified and harden it. In this way One is made from man and woman. —Büchlein von Stein der Weisen

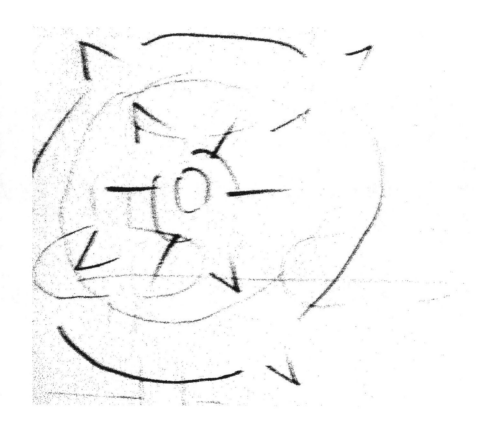

Archeus

The *Archeus* or soul of the world is the vital principle directing the growth and continuity of living beings through the soul's formative forces. The four ethers: warmth, light, chemical and life are incorporated in the *Archeus*; the functional aspects of attraction and repulsion, the sympathetic or antipathetic forces, draw out its essence. The degree of potency within the Will depends upon the Imagination's power to meet the *Archeus*.

•

Attenuated by Design

From the *prima materia* the active principle of extension endures into the four ethers: warmth, light, chemical and life. Individualized motive congeals into sense; the expressed motive is the object.

•

Biodynamic Imagination

What the plant world receives from mineral nutrition the human being receives through the senses. What the plant world receives from the sun, thinking receives from imagination.

Unconscious Light

Below consciousness the autonomic nerves coalesce image within the cosmically dark. Through this corrupted dynamism the senses reveal their actual images of the world.

·

Freeing Soul Into Feeling

World disposition constellates through feeling, suctioning time into blood. The chemical bath of cosmic *circulation* organizes the body of aeriform force into respiration, rhythmical projection and emotion. Throughout feeling, the *mysterium* inspires by exudation.

·

Imaginative Chemistry

By the properties and characteristics of substance, metabolic history and the under-conscious reach toward the *Potent Body*, rectifying impulse into Atmospheric Display.

•

Inside the Nuptial Chamber

By the amatory nature within *what* it does not yet possess, life-ether envelops cosmic-substance, developing the yearning of the cosmos in negative space. Out of this primal precipitate, physicality aspires into its form, discharging the ethers, enlivening the vaporous sweat, reflecting sensation. Pulled inside and liberated, these forces aren't simply given away. Slowly released by ignitions of sympathy and antipathy, the cocoon listens, the soul thickens.

•

Into Substance

Constituting the *lapis* has more to do with breathing than thinking, more so with willing than breathing. By the agency of the Arcanum destined into the terrestrial world, the way into substance is through depth of will.

•

Image Tasting

The *projection* suffers the generalized picturing of the world by *tasting* where the senses *cannot* go. The Work then carefully practices *not* going there.

•

Artfully Real

In his *De Auro* Pico cites five ways for producing gold by artificial means; he includes eighteen instances documenting its manufacture. Additional means for making gold are mentioned in the works of Nicolas Flamel, Gerhard Dorn and Jan van Helmont. However, it is solely in the present tense that gold can be generated by the Sun itself. This, by apprehending sunlight through the evaporation of afterimages.

•

Memory Elixir

Minerals from tone; bodies from light: condensation, incarnation. Pollens, oils, aromas rise while the life-ether positions earthward from cosmic periphery. The whole of heaviness bears into moment while ideation seeks the midday hour of existence. Between center and periphery the propensities of intelligence collect. Here births *relation, feeling* and *memory*, as metabolism becomes cosmic imagination freed into blood.

•

Mineral Abyss, Mineral Application

Mercury-silver-copper-gold conduct body into space. *Gold-iron-tin-lead* conduct time into spatial-thought. Gold joins space and thought in pure mineral *Byss*.

•

New Matter In the Present Tense

Time sheds into body within matter. Spirit articulates the fore-moment while intoning the everlasting. Married together they articulate the present tense.

•

Orienting Morphology

As the number seven symbolizes all that is transitory, the tetrad seeks repose. Contiguous with its sense for heaven, the will crosses the threshold into bodily form. Into the body, heaven enters diatonically, matter exits by way of the void.

•

Ouroboros and Surfactant

As *ouroboros* fashions the sense world, the sloughed-off skin develops into a literalized enchantment of time. Reassembling surface, porosity releases transparence from this corpse. Embracing this renewed "outside" succeeds in shedding surface into *manufactured* time.

•

Projection for a New Beginning

The plutonic springboard recoils from deep underworld, advancing toward un-hatched light. To discover the source of this yearning the viscera must necessarily be turned inside out. Here, eternity swallows sight into vision. Here, one comprehends that no limits can be set for devotion.

•

Insurgency and Devotion

For evolving the *astrum*, the soul's relation to sensing requires the commensurate development of inner chemistry. With the *albedo*, the whiteness, washing away impurities that hinder insight relieves the work of fallen salts and the manifold shadow projections.

•

Albedo

Foreshadowed throughout the perceptual realm is the projectively porous, through which images are washed in the bath of radiance. Readying the soul, reflection is proportional to the inclination of the in-breath, an impulse from the midnight hour of existence.

•

Prima Materia Moreover

It has been said of the first matter that it can be found everywhere but those unaware cannot see it. The *external* is discovered through the force of what digestion means. Matter first reveals itself *negatively*.

•

Steiner On the Stone

"You may read today about the Philosopher's Stone which was sought in an epoch when understanding of the nature of substances was very different from what it is today. And again, those who write about alchemy assert that nothing is known about the Philosopher's Stone. Here and there in my lectures I have said that this Philosopher's Stone is quite familiar to most people, only they do not know what it really is or why it is so called. It is quite well known, because as a matter of fact it is used by the ton."

•

Primary Matter Prefigures Touch

The spirit is touched by how the Ardent intuits primary matter as being caught in its own *compression*: captive, unable even to yearn for syntax.

•

Projection Through Contraction and Expansion

Modulating the aspirations of self, heat and will, the metals entrain toward a fluid state. Further, in wish for humanization, metals vaporize out of the aura of the ether-body. Contacted as intuitive form, substance renovates by negations. Through constituting its own meaning, the transparent is unequivocal satisfaction.

•

Coagulation By Invagination

Invaginating the infra-sensory radiance of cosmic imagery, the imagination enjoys coagulating the supra-conscious carried upon Hermes' wings *from* the future.

•

Arcanum-concept

Spirit is the *peripherally within* projecting the sum of the unknown.

•

Another Projection and Conduction

From outside, the *Potent Body* suctions the inner sense organization. From inside, the will conducts dimensionality to geometrical satisfaction. *As outside, so within.*

•

According to the Astrum

The nutritive soul is directed toward the metabolism according to the degree of *atman's* traction. This traction redirects the intention of the work toward an image. Here, nutrition is guided by the decaying cosmos as the heavenly offers itself to digestive purpose

Alchemical Process

Before the agency of the *lapis* can be engaged to rectify the body, a *dissolution* first re-members matter back to its condition on Saturn. Here, the blackening and putrefying of the corpse is eventually volatized and whitened by the lightening of Jupiter. Fixating the material through the force of Mars is the next step in the transformation. At this juncture, the *cauda pavonis* irradiates the sense bath by the powers of Mercury while the work readies to place Moon into Earth. Inside Earth, darkness renews. As this new carbonate must distill through philosophic milk, the organs of Venus triumph, producing the *extractum*.

Into a rarified *digestion* the Sun suckles the extract; expanding to *manas*, the air ferments into *buddhi*. While the *magnification* balances the spirit-life, refreshed warmth radiates the *projection* of imponderability. Deep within, the new Atmosphere potentizes through *atman* refracting the transfigured Saturn.

Cultivating the Quality

The being of nitrogen is the imagination of *manas*. Here the Art meets Isis-Sophia in nature. For accurate sense experience, the work cultivates the qualities in urine.

•

The White Lion

Archetypal cosmic substance—hydrogen—springs outward, away from earth. Generally warm and combustible, the white lion forms a ring, a mane of the nigh insubstantial.

•

Red Earth

Released for planetary consciousness, as iron accepts warmth and copper warms iron the constellation of the senses reclaims substance. In the *rubedo* dawn and dusk are thresholds to the nuptial chamber.

•

Rotational Mathematics

Within the consciousness soul *manas* rotates its spherical geometry into the construction of the destiny body. The *Potent Body* spins the force of Adam Caedmon into the art of the Unknown.

Schooling the Iron

Exercising the skin of percepts, digested thoughts project the horizon. Illumining the senses, the horizon of soul is reflexively forged from vivified iron. This tempering in the furnace of *buddhi* recollects the Black One, the shining Osiris. By steering Osiris' golden member to rejoin the abyss, creation is schooled by way of creating.

Circulatio

Quickening cosmic forces through rhythm and distillation, circulation renders, augments and exalts substance. *Circulatio* lifts matter's potential through repeated elevation, gently heating the mother tincture into gas, condensing air back into fluid. Satisfactorily potentized and spiritualized, this substance itself elucidates the *Archeus*.

Stirring the Queen's Motives

Nuptial imagery excites the ardor within the Queen's motives. Its projections stir material possession while impregnating the future with reformed cause.

·

How Vaporous Sweat Gains Form

Unsettled by connected portions of dampness and warmth, air resolves to a sphere. Settled by cold and dryness, the sphere grows icy, eager, expressing outwards into a snowflake. Air succumbing to earth gains form by atmospheric sweat. Sweat crystallizing forms cosmic tension.

·

Clarifying Vapor

A forward moving snail produces a mucus that dries to a sheen; beeswax fastens the forces for well-being. In the field of hexagonal equilibrium, vital heat ripens the vapor of perception. Feeling secretes outward the image colors of green, rose, black and white, adjusting surface tensions. Deeper yet, radiated by the inner realm of the creative *Byss*, is the altogether cosmically decayed compound, stilled.

Pneumatic Circuit Projection

From the effusions of heaven heat is conveyed. The pneumatic soul activates from this matrix where the movement of air dictates space unfolding. At the periphery, dimension factually reveals the outline of the Self.

•

A Candid Guide For Solubility

- Suspending habit and compulsion is essential. Surrender the impulse to interject notions and opinions.
- Too far away from center or too close to the logical jeopardizes the Work. Use the inner ear to listen *within* the attention.
- Stillness, observation and intention sustain the vessel. Keep the heart aroused despite the clues uncovered by shortcomings.
- The spirit changes constantly; practice having no distractions.
- Fate is a planned affair; distillation creates the future condition.
- Making mistakes requires simply continuing the work. Earn the right to transform.
- Never let tenderness grow stale. Grace breathes within the Central Fire.
- Revelations may be unwrapped poisons.
- Concentrating *within* the elements, do not lean on them; maintain your own weight.
- Attitude affects the outcome as the *artifactual* manufactures the new Atmosphere.
- Seek help by unlimited waiting. Realize results by unlimited devotion.

·

Substance of the Incorruptible Body

A cone, a question, a heart and horizon: examine the intent growing porous, becoming the substance of cosmic wish. By elemental engineering an invisible womb admits appearances while dismissing mere images. Examine their potent noise when touching the circle with three arms.

·

The Astrum Suctions Outwards

By characterological impulse, the *astrum* suctions outwards as feeling streams into the metabolic soul. From the *substance* of sense refraction, will redefines cosmic structure. This is the basis of *manas*, individualization, and the destined shape of devotion.

·

Life Itself Is An Emanation

It so stands that many are not awake to certain laws and determinations: The saints have a certain time during which they may exist. A tree may begin again to bloom and bear fruit having been barren for twenty years. Metals may be preserved from rust, wood may be protected from rot; blood may be preserved a long while, if the air is excluded. Animals awaken from their winter sleep; flies, having become torpid from the cold, become nimble again when warmed. The fabulous halcyon becomes rejuvenated, its own substance renewed by drawing nutriment so may without any interruption receive the influence of the divine. The vehicle that forms the *matrix* consists of certain specified substances in which quintessential forces are contained in greater quantities than in others, and being so, can be more easily extracted. Such substances are especially melissa, and the human blood. If we could extract the fire of life from the heart and draw the quintessence out of inanimate things, we might continue to live . . . we might mend that which we have broken and may dissolve that which we have made. *[Translated and adapted from the notes of Paracelsus]*

•

Imagining Life-ether and Feeling Will

Where life appears, warmth, light and tone move feeling into substance, move Imagination into growth, activate destiny into time. In the womb, the egg invites the horizon. The splendor throughout prefigures the span of a lifetime.

•

151

Carbonic Acid

When burned, oxygen releases carbonic acid. Reentering world process through the out-breath, carbon grips oxygen, converting into carbonic acid. As the atmospheric source for the inner life's impressions, carbonic acid restrains imagery from settling into fixations, enabling the imaginative index. Released qualitatively, carbonic acid points up how far within the *lapis* the work has come.

•

The Metallic Unveiling

Thinking encounters inner nature as unconsciousness is *physically* uncovered. Metals unveil their inner nature as thinking *thinks* into the world. Satisfied, minerals speak through comic will.

•

Sweetness and Light

Spagyrically with suitable intention, the soul of the Work can take sugar into color, color into sugar.

•

The Emanating Bride

Warmth is fermented cosmic affection. From this, red sulfur is applied to lymph, then air, amnion and saliva. Uncovering the viscera, drawing vowels from bone, by brushing this mixture on the universal abdomen a portrait of the Bride emanates. Practice apprehending the will to rectify the gown of splendor. The longing within this Art is a prayer for Her image.

•

A Cement for Venus and Mars

To a bath of distilled water add a trace of copper sulfate. Stir counterclockwise until vortices appear, robust and enlivened. Repeat stirring, clockwise. Add extract of lemon balm and sublimated quartz; stir until the vortices display a rosy color. Continue stirring until the clockwise vortex emanates a viridian-like blue. A halo appears streaming toward center, shimmering iridescent copper hues. Repeat stirring while further enlivening the solution with extract of nettle and potentized iron. The vortices deepen into a rhythm of colors appearing to form into a drop. Expand and contract this drop over and over again; its halo shimmers until colorless. Expand this colorlessness until *tone* arises. Here, a cement forms through the gown of silence from its source in the soul. Properly rendered, this process demonstrates the chemical wedding.

•

Third Projection

Generated from the dimensional world, the arc of *projection* illustrates circulatory passion from a place of heavenly repose. By the arcing will, the viscera aspect one another, binding and loosening the body. In the alembic of distilled intent, by dissipating confusion, the projective fire melds the organs into a new star. This body unfurls the structure of limitless form.

•

Resolving Transparence

Suspension, peripherality, poise, motivation, concentration, effort, unlimited waiting: *artifactually* resolving the cosmos is the aim of porosity.

•

Conjugal Potency

By light and ash, warmth and wet, the four ethers ignite the potency of form and outline, effect and physics. Before life substance activates, its power must marry the *not-yet*, remembering as the not-yet waits to be born.

•

Conjunctio

Circulating the will *rhythmizes* the elements throughout the streaming blood. Salted ocean, a flame in which to sleep, iron fixes earth, copper-vapor rising. All converge in the index of the viscerally special fluid. Blood conjugates as the sum of all signatures terrestrial, exalts the harmony of the metabolically celestial.

•

Diagramming Earth's Complete Lover

Bearing the new Atmosphere, the *astrum*'s presence, history and fantasy bear time forwards as well as backwards. Future and the past conflate into the freshened fabric of feeling. Throughout the body, devotion forms a beautiful outline of the earth's complete lover.

·

Vade Mecum Hermeticum

If the Work progresses, new karma develops. If there is no new work, nothing new develops.

Aqua ardens: by the chemistry of potent causes *putrefaction* delivers the corrosive power for unveiling appearances.

Deepening the feeling requires deepening the will, which provides the way through substances. To sharpen the senses, there must be willed intimacy placed into substances.

To determine the remedy discern which potency rules the pathology. For heaviness, the work stays below the diaphragm; for rhythmical dysfunction, it remains in the chest; to be a mirror for the light, it seeks the light. Low potencies address vitality; higher potencies address form.

By the actions of chemistry, within the soul's retort and its three-body influence, the *Arcanum* intends the *Potent Body*; such is the chemistry of unconfused projection.

Metals make base; oxides make sour; acids sour substances; salt travels through the earth.

"*Someone burned, someone burns.*" A salt cannot be distilled out, yet it may be vaporized.

There are three imaginal diaphragms: one diaphragm between the head and the chest, another between the chest and the abdomen, a third in the region of the pelvis. Laterality and polarity must be taken into consideration in order to arrange a conversation between the upper and lower, the right and left, the soul and the physical.

The head organizes the self and the *sense for* meeting sensation. The head contains the polarity of male and female, hence the head presents both Venus and Mars as forces within past karma pressed into the upper sphere.

From the solid aggregate of matter, light-ether is derived. Catabolism creates as a by-product the imponderable element of light-ether; the Venus organs excrete the material while they spiritualize through light-ether.

Contrast that which offers itself in the processes of tin-Jupiter to those of copper-Venus. Consider these pairings: Mars and Venus are in close relation to the ether body. Mercury and Jupiter are close to the astral body. Moon and Saturn to the warmth body, the *I*.

Through our recognition of the new Saturn impulse we come to identify our capacity for enlivened thinking through the heart, a stimulation of soul warmth.

Magnification is the process of extraction expanded into the horizon of the invisible.

Through death, resurrection and light-ether are connected with catabolism, with Venus and the kidneys.

Distillation must also take into account a certain amount of stability necessary for substance to remain as substance.

The zodiac rings around the skull as the spleen digests iron. The cerebellum observes digestion through the heart.

If the ether is too weak, the warmth gets too strong; illness is the consequence.

If the *digestion* does not conquer the character of the substance, the substance will conquer the body.

In principle, one seeks to assuage *the double* so to harmonize proper incarnation.

Curative processes are conversations between the iron phantom and the silver moon force. If remedies can't heal, iron will heal; if iron doesn't heal then warmth will heal; if warmth doesn't heal then the disease is not curable.

The Principalities ignite motion and time—the love-impulse for enthusiasm. The Work gathers its devotion first through attraction, followed by wish, after that the fruits of transparence.

Within the earth, extraction; within water, infusion; within air, decoction; within fire, distillation. These actions are utilized for crystallizing the root, ashing the stem, digesting the leaf, potentizing for the flower, sublimating for the oil, carbonizing for the seed.

Celestial gardening is not without its own progression. In winter, the Ardent must store his thoughts below the ground to obtain the favors of earth's awakened spirits.

The iron-phantom provides the foundation for the cosmic-metallic forces to enter the body. If the iron phantom is damaged, these forces cannot enter.

The *Arcanum* reconciles the iron phantom and the lunar plateau. Through porosity the *Potent Body* furthers the *Great Inoculation*.

In the chemistry of transparent causes, history ripens into fruit. Through the course of *magnification*, time is re-educated into sweetness.

The Work must inquire where the "wound" lives, and how the soul's activities are "fixated." In the balance between thinking, feeling and willing one finds love. The task taken up by the Art is love-*doing*, strengthening the cocoon for metamorphosis.

Says Hermes Trismegistus in the *Tabula Smaragdina,* "Its power is perfect if it is changed into earth."

The platonic solid of the octahedron represents the air element in light-ether. For applying the elocutionary force of the Work, pyrite (iron sulfite as an octahedron crystal) is of immense value.

Meteoric iron originates out of the cosmos, arming into the activity of the limbs, freeing the voice, paving the path for transparence to be experienced.

Lightening relieves the pressure of the atmospheric heaviness, clearing the air as it produces nitric oxide and ultimately nitric acid. Lully prepared a corrosive for silver by heating niter and clay, calling it *aqua fortis*, a corrosive for "clearing out" substance. The practical aspects of separating the moon forces out from Venus and the Sun forces allows for a counter-reproductive "engraving," surface developing another *outside*. Differently, the royal water of *aqua regia* refines *aurum* into pure gold precipitate: the Sun is made more earthly through digesting warmth into *spontaneity*.

To understand the Work, one must live in relationships. See the bee, and how she differs from the ant, the wasp, and especially the spider. See the whelk and how it is similar to the cochlea.

The pelvis senses imbalance, especially in the relation to earth and oxygen. It stands under the auspices of the moon providing a capacity to reflect the pathological events in the Work. Stirring the Work with resins in the activated atmosphere of petrichor gives it balance, furthering the life-sense.

The poison of bees is that of the ego-organization of the blood. Potassium and sodium are the ego organization of the intestines; silica, that of the skin.

The etheric has three messenger-kings: salt, mercury and sulfur. Utilize the New Arcanum as the principal diagnostic model, engage its messengers as the treatment. The work attends to how it is ruled by which of these, and for what each is meant.

The light-ether is derived from the inner carbon where the imponderable is a by-product. The process flows from water to air to warmth. What happens between water and air is terrestrial; between air and warmth, cosmic. The fallout of terrestrial activity is material; the reverberation of the cosmic is spiritual.

•

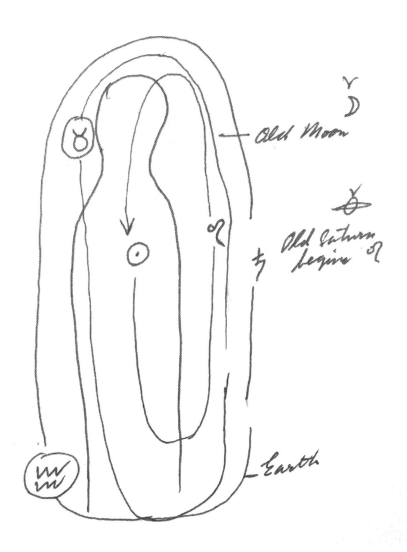

♈
☽

— Old Moon

♄

♌

— Old Saturn
begins ♌

— Earth

phys vortex toward center
etheric vortex center outward

Assembling the Artifactual Spirit

Solve for who you will be, for flesh to become melody. —The Bride's Hermetic rhyme

D 30

29
28   Light

D 27   Fire

salt

21
20

merc   18
                        17   Air
                 D13   D 14
         D13   D 13

sal
         ♀
                 D 7
         D 6

                              water

         ☉   D 1   Earth

Projective Creation

Through its relationship to bodily *releasement*, intentionality increases the potential of the Atmosphere. By the soul of intentionality, consequences free out of indeterminacy, from disposition into *Display*.

•

Potent Body

The history of formative force is encountered in the physical coalescing of body. Within the *memory-elixir* the *Archeus* emanates perceptible transparence. Activated Imagination is blood engaging on the level of the Arcana, not that of fluid.

•

Suspensions, Solutions, Aperture: Magnification and Review

By the Gradual Dispersion the body evokes, the psyche involves. The firmament acts as a fulcrum between enchantment and resistance. About this fulcrum heat evolves.

Seeing causes as caught between two hard places reclaims them.

Consider again, why could there be a problem with awareness? Why does the thrust of awareness eventually reflect upon itself?

Toward exterior warmth, the precipitate cradles its filaments, enervates its waves.

Longing for what it knows yet cannot imagine, for what does the *astrum* yearn?

The senses exist to illustrate depth of field. Depth of field is the *given-over*.

Through the eyes there is a suction that employs a sensory digestion. By the grace of the iris space opens to savor.

Vision and creation are one. Light is not to be confused with sunlight.

Scents mesh to inform the field of the primal *sensorium.* Through olfaction odors intone the chords of metabolism. While matured sensation increases its discriminatory faculty, unripe impressions rest in the senses as if the sensible were a certain *place*.

While there are those who incline to think outward, the Ardent aspires to will inward.

With the work in suspension, noticeable about the will is its holiness and its shallowness. Virgin and fornicator, perverse for all existence. Rather than shedding light on itself, the will draws upon its own source.

Will is the dream-plasma of the Hierarchies. Intending the will etches the soul; character thus becomes the formative divine awakening.

The Art's operation is a projective cross: a heart and a horizon, a cone and a question.

Transparent and limitless, the divine is the horizon in three planes. The transparent is all heart and it can be shown.

166

The theophanic twin offers its face through the force of the *I* meeting annihilation and aspiration.

The face of that angel from which is apprehended *relation* is a very secret face, a face whose motions join *before* and *after* time.

The character of the moon harbors retarded spirits. Of note is the activity of those whose thinking lodges in the viscera.

Unwrapping the mummification wrought by fear, it is appropriate to dread thoughts that may not pass directly through the body. They can, if given the chance, STOP inside the viscera.

Fear is the adverse chemical *mumia*. By distilling those fears most central to the Coagulate the turbid may become intelligible, the shaking blood may become steadied.

Metamorphosing fear within the suction of the *astrum,* the cultivation of heart forces—*cardiopoeisis*—is a permeation into the not-yet, time as time is coming to be.

Expecting nourishment, bellies grow empty. Dreaming the milky *Archeus* the body is nourished. Ingesting memories and theogonies, the body must withstand the cracks under the interstitial weight.

The Work is populated with names whose essence is exuded between the gods and stones.

Like lactation and blessed sperm, the *Ignition* is the admixture of two feelings; the first rests in the sentiment of *home,* the other is restless, needing to wander.

Heredity has become a nightmare the blood must learn to wash away. History will succumb to purified surfactants.

Shifting the inner horizon toward uprightness, the ground becomes the first construction for the ability to de-sensitize to physical life. Thus, the ground can be suckled with the feet by the arches, forming by a vacuum of primal levity. In this way, one stands as the progeny of the gods.

Wonder reflexes connectivity; contact attunes to what lies hidden, extended outward. Through touch, wonder is made palpable. Ever since the beginning, wonder re-penetrates the Spirits of Form.

By halting the potential of the senses beyond sensing process, the *astrum* fixates surface.

Primary sensing is reabsorbed into the unconscious. However, there is a portion given over, released into the world as an "object" of memory, a mummification of the unobserved, overlooked, hidden.

Beauty is gestated within wisdom dismissing a conceptual end to the world.

By elemental engineering beauty births an invisible womb, a womb to *save* this world.

Love through the senses, love through the elements. Love precipitates war and letting blood. As such, trouble worships love as it disinherits fate.

By the law of transparence, as gold completes substance, so the Divine becomes the created.

The substance of the incorruptible body generates the cosmos' ignition. The given-over *is* love.

Dressed in encaustic purple: the sun within an aureole of honeycomb.

Through the qualities of perception, phenomena radiate irrepressibly. On the other hand, freeing phenomena through sense-free action *liberates them.*

Love learns its finer art through transparence. Those freed into transparence produce the ovum of the future. Within the inner firmament, the history of habits is available for disappearing.

168

Though immense in scope and progression, heaven nevertheless changes.

The tongue is the distillation for *how* anything and everything can be said. By the activity of speech, thoughts are made possible.

Mental pictures, as they play upon the nerves, are *a* conclusion of the world.

Wakefulness through materialized intellection *destroys* the world. How long until all form turns to dust? How long until all dust regains form?

Intuition raises the catalytic ferment, the motions of emotion *infolding* the will-body.

Longing into the metallic mist, there is no end to dissolving into transparence else eternity becomes a vast prison.

Bone marrow harbors the Central Fire. Outside the body, circumstance is the subject of the marrow's blood making.

The etheric body is set in rhythmic motion by the character of the sun's formative force; it is not a body of form, rather, a *body of motion.*

As the blood swims in the will, blood becomes the vehicle for cosmic implosion.

True for substance: fire makes new forms by destroying blood, makes new blood when destroying old forms.

Much of the future is written at the moment of death. Conscious death is a mindful deed, a preparation for awareness in rebirth.

Prior to physical death, the flow of blood must *not* be stopped before its forces depart for the cosmos.

•

How Many Radii?

By the *astrum*, the senses induct substance: instilling the world within by inspiring the outside. For *making sense* the soul battles becoming exclusively substance or solely function. Stirred by the Central Fire, the soul displays direction, placement, formative force, movement and disposition. The soul's radii involute the world through the twelve senses while its center refracts it.

•

First Hermes, Second Hermes

Emanation shrouds formative force, reflection unfurls its influence. Insofar as motives develop substance, substances envelop motives: imaginative perception coagulates the first Hermes. Turning percepts inside out, motives within substance release their vaporous sweat. This urge toward the periphery releases the second Hermes. By will-force turned *inside out*, intuition becomes the god.

•

Directing Radiance

Suspending time, willing backwards purifies the chthonic image by disassembling the outward motion of impulse. In this moment, radiance follows the soul correcting its course.

•

Constituting New Surface

Between the metabolism's anabolic assembly and the sense's embrocation, substance directs concentration into congealment. Upon *surface* actions leave a genuine trace as the cosmos imbibes the record of all affairs.

•

Conducting Fire

Four principal colors are displayed through the Work: black, white, yellow, and red. These educate for the handling of fire. As well, they show the onset and duration of the first, second, and third fires of the Work. In the Work, colors themselves instruct what there is to do.

•

Secondary Inspiration

Heaven rejoices as transparence threads the *iliaster* into the *Potent Body*. In this magnified respiration, Inspiration displays diffracted porosity. The anatomy of the new *mysterium* displays carbon conducted, color configured, signatures revised.

•

Reassembling the Image

Perceiving the life-breath within feeling, the Ardent visualizes the mythic imagery of world process. This projective distillate sees the gods within perception prior to perception becoming wholly nerve-sense based.

•

Syntactic and Periphery

Before birth, the soul anticipates its organic syntax. After death the body rectifies its grammar. The living evaporate as the dead enliven. Such is the inversion of heaven. Through this the spirit assembles the Self.

•

Active Perception and the Luminous Frontier

Salt reflects the luminous in the frontier within sensing. Sulfur decays itself within the factual body. Together, this decay and horizon invite the cosmic radii inward. Inside the clear alembic this longing for sweetness becomes *sweetness*.

•

The Objective of the Breath

Within *atman* primordial subjectivity once yielded cosmic hysteria. Its destined objective excitedly instructs the periphery required for the future metamorphosing of physical existence.

•

Infinity Spins On Air

Loosened by the sensible perception from the inner realm and reconfigured by the thorax, the organs evolve their inner ellipses toward the planets, onwards toward the zodiac. Throughout supersensory dimension, the spine's axis joins the vastness of Adam Caedmon.

•

The Radiant Medium

Heat: the first medium. From heat, so the heart's emanations. When the heavens constituted their dynamism for assembling the heart, the effectual radiation became the cosmos' crucial means. As well, its crucial aim.

•

Mercurius Vivus

For the blood's circulation, the intention stills yet purposively wanders. The world periphery inverts as the heart is created. Reversed, inmost

174

activity shapes itself for the cosmic periphery; every pull toward the horizon coagulates a new center. Here, Mercury is a great conductor; though he may abandon the whole for the part, his sphericity is never incomplete.

·

On Manufacture

Overcome by undue heaviness or wanton ignition, the breath of the *astrum* at times bewilders creation. Worldly light fails as confusion draws in false carbon. For the Atmospheric inoculation, the *Potent Body* breathes clarity into the four principle gases. In reanimated carbon, respiration and circulation reach into Imagination, this, as the heart of circulation manufactures the new Atmosphere.

·

Mineral Sense and the Lapidum Philosophorum

A threefold confluence inheres within each of the elements. Fructifying the intentions of mercury, salt and sulfur identifies the individuality of substance. Through the mineral realm the will breathes into sense, marrying porous intent, humanizing substance. Light taken to air allows mineral sense to exhale the philosophic stone.

●

Carbonic Awakening

Intention reawakening within carbon: this is the universe's most radical gesture.

●

From Inspiration to Unbornness

Physicality flows into sense by the Arcanum; the senses flow into sense-consciousness by the *astrum*. Taking image-making into living thinking requires fixing spirit *against* sense, placing matter into the heart of its own null point. The whole of the self is inverted inspiration.

●

The Visceral Future

The sense organs are constituted to coalesce form as the brain and nerves reflect imagery. Digesting world motives, sensation reflects imaginative destruction back into the stars. Lastly, by annihilating exteriority the viscera blossom.

•

As Carbon, So Planetary Love

Carbon shapes the etheric effusions into placement. Entering red, earth assembles fertility; emitting blue, serenity assembles heaven. Together, true sleep assembles the inner Arcanum. Within the dreaming carbon, inside the heart of the cosmos, awakened sleep activates the Elixir. As sleep, so the awakened power of re-membering. As carbon, so love.

•

Blood Is A Distillate From the Future

Evaporating images involves instilling the future through adjusting the arterial spray. Conversely, physical images grotesquely metamorphose mental pictures; they surface by antipathy to pre-natal existence, and further by their antipathy an imagination of the cosmos itself.

•

Cauda Pavonis Resorbed

The Ardent marries space through combustion, solution, digestion, distillation. When the *cauda pavonis* resorbs this luster, the new uterus opens. Deep within: congealment, separation, reflection, potentization. The will of porosity enters darkness, then exits from the heart as substance and medium become one.

•

On the Shedding of Metals

As time continues to be misunderstood, the metals further condense. Wherever time continues being bred there one observes the metals continually being shed.

•

Mineral Sense Into Lapis, Lapis Into Nitrogen Sense

From instinct to living tone, blood lifts the dust of existence into the air of the Atmosphere. The embryonic *buddhi* inhales the already-dead, the awakened carbon of the out-breath. Braiding death into devotion, the senses respire, releasing *spirit-life*.

•

Adam Caedmon Sprung

Iliaster's primordial radii push from center to crown, from crown to extremity. Pole to periphery, metabolism expands, powered by extension from the head downward. Fastened by gravity, the Firmament stirs ahead of sensation.

•

As Gold Becomes Everything

Gold establishes its artifactual presence within chemical sight; by the law of transparence the divine becomes the created.

•

Turning to Mist

By *manas* the cosmic will magnifies the senses, entraining the world's wishes, multiplying *artifactual* splendor. Turning to mist, *atman* pares the skin of the heavens, hanging it upon its corpuscular light.

·

Through the Reign of Dissolution

After the head gives to the earth the contents of life's distillate, feeling readies to evolve new circulation. Feeling substance continually evaporates carbon, shedding emotion and thought into the unfixed atmosphere. Through the reign of dissolution, the metabolism takes up this chaos into the destiny of regenerated light.

·

Artifact and Display

Matter divests its tendency to decay away from the *artifactual* spirit through the construction of the *Potent Body*. Breathed out by vivid carbon, the Atmosphere *displays* the body restoring itself in death.

·

Released From Red Earth

While the viscera house karma within the depths of metabolism, illumined sleep awakens *will*. By raising the under-conscious, *buddhi* reveals organic presence hidden within the inter-*in*active sphere of physicality. Cleansing the viscera of accumulated oblivion, within awakened sleep the threshold of illumination is crossed.

•

Lapis and Digestive Motive

The nutritive realm enters the imponderable where the motives of light meet the structure of the cosmos. As the cosmos admits the will of the Ardent, the *lapis* is digested to the highest degree. This gold is no ordinary gold.

•

Raising Into Light

Though the body coagulates and densifies, the viscera are capable of being trained to disperse their weight. As the *astrum* is guided toward reversing pressure, the negative pressure, a vacuum of the *Archeus*, edifies substance in order to marry cosmic life.

Magnified Into the Present

With *magnification* the practice does not dread death, a surety of material destiny, nor does it dread the imagery of the transition to death. Initiated, the work's fortitude infuses with the present tense "experience" of death, instilling a nexus of the accumulated time-body, altering death-time in regards to both life-time and prior *unbornness*.

•

Aqua Regia

Care must be given to differentiate solution from error, initiation from counter-initiation. The skill for genuinely dissolving gold provides the necessary dynamic. Dissolving gold illustrates the aptitude for the required resolve, which is not unlike the capacity to apprehend time in liquid form. As an extraction without distillation, this pure "tinge" lives by the potency of insight, by the art of drawing spirits, by the key to the twelve labors.

•

Visita Interiora Terrae Rectificando Invenies Occultum Lapidem

Calculus albus, calculus candidus, lapis noster, lapis occultus, Adamus, Aer, Animalia in excelsis, Alkahest, Antidotus, Antimonium, Aqua benedicta, Aqua volans per aeram, Arcanum Atramentum, Autumnus, Basilicus, Brutorum cor, Capillus, Capistrum auri, Carbones, Cerberus, Chaos, Cinis cineris, Crocus, Dominus philosophorum, Draco elixir, Filius ignis, Fimus, Folium, Frater, Granum, Granum frumenti, Haematites, Hepar, Kyrios, Lac, Choler, Melancholia, Ovum philosophorum, Panacea salutifera, Phlegmatikos, Phoenix, Pyrites, Radices arboris solares, Regina & Rex regum, Sal metallorum, Salvator terrenus, Sanguineus, Sulfuris, Tetrad, Ventus hermetis.

•

Light and Active Light

Lifted from its source *inside* the imponderables, passive light arises. The Arcanum emanates life before light. So where does light come from? Of what is it composed? Beyond the zodiac is another world, the *Byss*, where active life suckles through the opaque.

•

Time-Assemblage

Disassembled by transparence, the future intones inside the Celestial Ear. The auditorium of *artifactual* space is a *religion* of time as time is coming to be.

•

Light and Sublimated Gold

The philosopher Robert Fludd announced, "Light is sublimated gold, rescued magically by invisible stellar attraction, out of material depths." As well, this sublimated gold is unveiled by means of the surface tension evaporated through transparence.

•

The Physical Body Etherized

Celestial resolve inheres in the exponential sleep of mineral consciousness. The mineral assembles its identity through refracted spirit. Exposed, the mineral is the agent of silence, pure potential in dynamic repose. Through *inverted longing*, the other-side of existence expires the potency of surface, instates material elocution, activates the *silence* assimilating mineral residue.

·

Preliminary for the Birth to Come

Its potential dynamically charged, homeopathically the head enjoys decapitation. Cast off, the head is the herald of the new precipitate, a remedy for the center of the world. Inside out and released, the head becomes what is thought-through.

·

Assembly and Disappearance

As intestines, lungs and tongue imbibe the projective force of history, the body pulls form from fire. By redirecting the inverted Firmament, body and surface are suspended into the luminous frontier. Reformed, mineral surface awakens by sensation.

·

Atmospheric Delight

In the midday hour of existence the Atmosphere infuses into the individualized powers of projection and restraint. The work balances the *astrum* in the sphere of porosity. Resolving confusion, heaviness and radiance prove the body of Hermes.

•

New Substance (New Gods)

Matter is the end point of spirit, the horizon waiting. As heaven delights in capitulating new designs, with new work is born new substance.

•

By This Constitution

Transparence is a fact of cosmic imagination. Telluric darkness invaginates cosmic wish. In resisting the *prima materia*, sensation constitutes the active periphery where but *one* god has gone before.

•

Disappearance and Gold

Maturing matter requires extracting the spirit from Saturn, soul from Sun. After procuring the fruit of the elements, the chemical body must be watered by Hermes and warmed by the Bride. Ripened, gold lives imponderably within its own disappearance.

•

A Chemical Moment

As cosmic forces draw forth the body, the absorption of the sense world conditions individualized warmth, the visceral organs, the blood. Metabolically, in the depths of sleep, cosmic will orients toward the *not-yet* with instinctual bearings.

As the will "awakens," embracing the peripheral imagination, sensation dreams like a surfactant into the forces of warmth, air, moisture and mineral. World content meets the periphery of the sensing body while the primacy of perception is birthed through the soul's applied feeling for substance.

Between sense and will, the admixture of idea and substance dissolves throughout the chemical atmosphere. The residue from dampened primary heat gradually cools, hollows out as a conduit of possibility, of awareness.

The breath of awareness builds the embryonic force for vision. With individualized will, bodily vision fructifies within the atmospheric womb. Here, the recognition of the Atmosphere appears as light absorbed by the Bride, delineating and reflecting the Ardent's own light.

Reflectively, the ether becomes a body of perception whose goal is exact vision. By Her gown of blue, the Imagination seeks the Arcana of all things. By Her guiding intent, the *mysterium* gradually unveils.

Infused from the microcosm's limitless devotion, the *mysterium* of the Arcana is received into the body. Here increases the great work distinguishing chemical intent. "In the great relationships of the cosmos, illusion is a necessity." Illusion is the driving force for the *artifact* to evolve. In the alembic of purified sleep, distillation refracts the shadow of substance displaying the *embryo* prior to substance.

If illusion moves too far inward, the Atmosphere ignites into smoke. Too far outward, the Atmosphere hardens into salt.

The source of light itself shows the body of formative force through its own projection into Imagination.

The work is time-based, specific, portraying the inner *astrum* of the microcosm. Here, the ferment steeps, ripening while sloughing off distorted light and insufficient air.

In the primal spirit force of light lives creative thought; within love lives the creative will. Self-will initiates into the Groom, world-will into the Bride. Brought into mutual attraction, the will prepares for its chemical marriage to light.

As the art upholds the depths of understanding, the Bride is the figuration of the supersensible. "Love is the only soul force that can remain unchanged when the soul enters the spirit world."

•

Lapis Lingua

liberating the skull
the placement of dissolution
by lead, silver, nose
the raven, the silkworm
the felicities of projection
through thorax and limbs
texture and darkness
gem of Maris
star of the sea
cleansed breath through misty Tartarus

lapis lingua
relaxed into tone
darkness stretched
from the extended body of form
unlocking carbon
condensed through retort
the Atmosphere potentizes
lapis, speaking

•

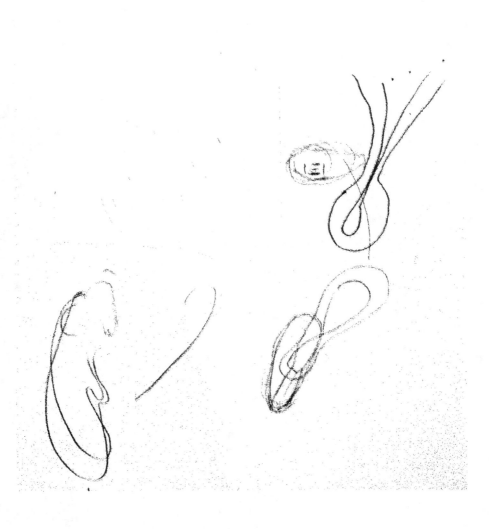

Chemically, Our Mother

Our Mother,
Handmaiden to identity
Hallowed be your pains,
Thy fruit is come
As our lives are done
Through this offering
As it is in heaven.

Give us this day
Your porous breast
That we may uphold the Potent Body.
Relieved into *the excitement to exist*
We deliver Creation's wish to you,
For now what lives is
Afar all ecstasy and power:
Our atmospheric heart
Exalting your chemical song.

A philosopher and homeopath, Andrew Franck has worked closely with a number of renowned researchers and physicians such as Otto Wolff, Klaus Wilde and Alfred Tomatis. His writings include *The Transparent Bride*, *The Art of Porosity*, *Projective Mythology* and *The Alchemical Circus*. He is director of The Healing Arts, a holistic health facility, and the Center for Imaginative Studies, both in Woodstock, New York.

www.theartofporosity.net